COMPANY COMMAND

The Bottom Line

COMPANY COMMAND

The Bottom Line

JOHN G. MEYER, JR.
Major General, USA

1996

Byrrd Enterprises, Inc.
1302 LaFayette Drive
Alexandria, Virginia 22308
1-800-628-0901
FAX: 1-703-768-4086

John G. Meyer, Jr.
Major General, USA

First published in the USA by the National Defense University Press 1990.

Published with the permission of the author by:

Byrrd Enterprises, Inc.
1302 LaFayette Drive
Alexandria, VA 22308
1-800-628-0901
FAX: 1-703-768-4086

BYRRD ENTERPRISES, INC. publications are sold by BYRRD ENTERPRISES, INC.

Opinions, conclusions and recommendations expressed or implied within are solely those of the author and do not necessarily represent the views of the National Defense University, the Department of Defense, the Congressional Research Service, or any other Government agency.

To The Soldier

On The Importance of Company Command

A company commander is charged with a sacred trust: The lives of his soldiers, men and women he may be called upon to lead in combat. There's no greater trust that can be bestowed by the American people than a personal responsibility for the lives of their sons and daughters. . . .

Company command, if it is successful, is the most rewarding, personally satisfying position the Army offers. It provides a young officer a fundamental knowledge, experience, and a sense of capability that will serve him well the rest of his Army career. If he can command a company properly, he'll be able to command a battalion, brigade or division. *Successful* company command is an absolute prerequisite for subsequent success in the Army.

General Frederick J. Kroesen

Contents

Foreword

Taking command at any level is an exhilarating opportunity, usually leavened by a modicum of uncertainty. At no time is this more true than during an officer's *first* command, for this is when young men and women take up the mantle of command without the background and experience of more senior officers. At few other times do officers need practical guidance so urgently as during that first command.

Many manuals address the general principles of leadership, and scores of books recount the lives of famous leaders, but rare is the volume that addresses the crucial issues of first command. Rarer still is the volume that speaks frankly to its audience, providing a full array of concrete information, anecdotal illustration, and "Dutch-uncle" advice. *Company Command: The Bottom Line* by Major General John G. Meyer, Jr., is such a book. It begins with the important matter of assuming command properly, and then goes on to explain how to establish correct relationships within the company and battalion chains of command. Ensuing chapters show how best to deal with legal, personnel, training, supply, maintenance, and a host of other matters. Major General Meyer enriches the book at every step with pointers, examples, and senior-officer comment—conveniently highlighted as "Tips," "War Stories," and "What the Brass Says."

Although written by an Army officer primarily for Army company commanders, this book has considerable information, suggestions, and insights that are directly applicable to other services. Indeed, there is much in it that first-line supervisors in non-military organizations will find easily adaptable to their situations. This refreshingly written guide may well turn out to be one of those books not to be read only once, but one to keep at hand for ready reference.

J.A. Baldwin
Vice Admiral, US Navy
President
National Defense University

Preface

I wrote this book to help lighten the load of one of the most overworked soldiers in the US Army—**THE COMPANY COMMANDER**. It is commonplace for military leaders to call a company commander's job the hardest job in the Army. Company commanders have more to do in one day than they can ever accomplish. A company commander works ten to twelve hours a day, six or seven days a week, and refers to over 100 manuals and documents—just to stay ahead of the proverbial power curve.

Despite the time and stress, successful company command is the most rewarding job in the Army.

Company Command: The Bottom Line spells out, for the first time, the **essential** tasks a company commander must complete and shows how he or she should perform them in order to command successfully. It's not a book on leadership, nor is it a book that includes everything a company commander does—although much in it applies to leadership and the many burdens of command. It's a concise, practical reference that will help make a "rookie" commander a "pro."

The book is written for any unit, regardless of mission. Although I concentrated on company command in the Active Forces, this book's general principles and most of the concrete details and specific references apply equally to command in Guard and Reserve units. We are, and always will be, one Army.

It's written for the worst case: You have your own orderly room, budget, motor pool, supply room, and so forth; and you have **real** problems to deal with. Read this book and it will—

- Start you off running when you take command.

- Identify your most important tasks and tell you how to complete them.
- Show you how to set new directions for your company.
- Challenge you to think and solve typical company commander problems.
- Give you confidence to command with authority.
- Arm you with previously unpublished tricks of the trade.
- Make you a better commander.

If you have time to read only one book prior to assuming command, read this one. Read it as a platoon leader and as an incoming commander. Then use it as a reference while in command. Give it to others to read—to your lieutenants, and especially to your first sergeant. He needs to buy into chapter 3, "You and Your First Sergeant."

The book is arranged so that each chapter addresses one particular command responsibility. So you can read all the chapters in order or use the book as a reference for "Dutch Uncle" advice about particular problems. You'll discover how many command responsibilities overlap and how solutions to command problems apply to many unrelated matters.

In case you need more information on a particular topic, each chapter contains its own references. Of course, reference titles and numbers of Army Regulations, Field Manuals, Department of the Army Pamphlets, and such publications may change or be superseded; therefore, double-check the current validity of the source before using it for official purposes.

This book is written in plain English and filled with TIPS, WAR STORIES, and QUOTES ("The Brass Says")—all designed to make company command a great experience for you and your soldiers.

TIPS—ways to do things smarter and more professionally. (You won't find these Tips in Army Regulations, Field Manuals, or other such publications.)

WAR STORIES—reflections of actual situations and how to do and not to do something.

THE BRASS SAYS—quotes from military leaders who've been in your shoes and commanded successfully.

This book comes from hundreds of hours of interviews and discussions with general officers, brigade and battalion commanders, company commanders (successful and unsuccessful), brigade and battalion command sergeants major, company first sergeants, and soldiers, and my own personal experiences. The ideas and ways of doing things are proven. Pick and choose those you feel comfortable with and become the best commander ever. This book is a guide, not a bible.

THE BOTTOM LINE: Company command is the greatest job in the Army. Do it right—right from the start.

Acknowledgments

When General John Wickham was Army Chief of Staff, he announced as one of his eight principles of leadership, "Make history—make a difference." I hope *Company Command: The Bottom Line* will make such a difference. The generous and sustained assistance and unflagging encouragement of a number of superb soldiers, caring leaders, and true friends made this book possible. To them I will always be indebted.

- To Mr. John Shannon, LTG Bradley Hosmer, LTG Andrew Chambers, MG Eugene Cromartie, MG Charles Hines, and COL Bill Ladd, COL Walt Ferguson, COL Jim Velezis, and COL Rich Goldsmith, your guidance helped focus the book.

- To my fellow students at the Industrial College of the Armed Forces (Class of 1988, and particularly section 9), I thank you for your ideas and input. LTC Rance Sopko's support as a "sounding board" was magnificent.

- To COL Paul O'Connell, LTC Steve Curry, MAJ Dave Carey, MAJ Doris Miller, Dr. Bill McCarron, Les Hunkele, and Ed Seneff, my NDU Press editor, my thanks for helping translate my ideas into "plain English." To Kurt Sanford, special thanks for your countless hours of critical editorial review and for always asking the hard questions.

- To Dr. Fred Kiley, your unwavering confidence, encouragement, and constant backing made this book a reality.

- To my daughter, Stephanie, and son, J.G., I thank you for your patience and understanding during this demanding ordeal; and to my wife, Mary, without your consideration, *total* support, and devotion, this book would not have been possible.

- To the reader—I know this acknowledgment section may read like a last will and testament, but always remember those who helped get you where you are today—for without them, you are nothing.

On Leading Soldiers

The American soldier, the finest fighting soldier in the world, deserves your steady leadership, your care, your compassion, and your genuine love. You will know when you have given sufficient measure of these qualities. You will know when you look into your soldiers' eyes, for it is there you will learn how they judge and respect you as a leader. In the end, you are a *TRUE* leader only when your leadership is ratified in the hearts of your soldiers.

General William J. Livsey, Jr.

COMPANY COMMAND

The Bottom Line

1. Who's In Charge?

You Are

And Don't Ever Forget It !

2. Taking Command

Leadership in a democratic army means firmness, not harshness; understanding, not weakness; justice, not license; humaneness, not intolerance; generosity, not selfishness; pride, not egotism.

General Omar N. Bradley

COMPANY COMMAND is the most *demanding* job in the Army. It's the toughest job you'll have as a captain, one of the toughest jobs you'll have during your career. Command *can* be lonely. But remember, you weren't selected to be a company commander to win a popularity contest. The Army selected you because you've shown you're a leader who has potential and can complete the mission.

The contributions you can make to the Army as a *good* company commander are infinite. As a commander you're a role model every minute of every day of your command. Soldiers need and want to be led; they look to you for guidance. Be a model. You'll cherish the rewards of successful command the rest of your life. Don't waste this opportunity to be the best company commander ever and to make a difference.

To Be or Not To Be a Company Commander?

Don't be insulted by this question: Why do you want to command? Is it because you want to lead soldiers? Or maybe you don't want the rigorous responsibilities of command, but you'll take the opportunity of future advancement if you succeed? For self-servers, command will not be a pleasant experience. They'll do their time, punch their ticket, make no impact, and then move on. Check out the questions on the next page to determine your desire to command:

- Are you willing to dedicate yourself 24 hours a day, seven days a week, if necessary, for your unit and your soldiers?
- Is your family willing to bear the sacrifices?
- Are you willing to lead by example in everything you do—to live in a fish bowl with your personal and professional life open to view?
- Are you a doer? Can you lead your company to excellence?
- Do you understand that loyalty is a two-way street?
- Can you challenge your soldiers to go the extra mile, knowing the challenges may increase, though the rewards remain the same?
- Are you willing to put your neck on the line and take risks when necessary?
- Are you willing to make the tough decisions, regardless of the consequences?
- Are you willing to take responsibility for everything that happens, or doesn't happen, in your unit?
- Are you willing to support your boss completely and wholeheartedly, even if he or she is not a person you like?
- Are you willing to sacrifice your career to protect and preserve the dignity of your soldiers?

Simply put, successful company command requires *total* dedication, energy, commitment, and support to your soldiers—anything less can hinder the mission and hurt your soldiers.

What It Takes to be a Successful Company Commander

It's time for plain language. You "gotta" try to be many things to all your soldiers, all the time. Successful company command is judged not by your report card, but by service and loyalty to your soldiers and your commander. The following "you gottas" are essential for success:

YOU GOTTA WANT IT: You must have the desire, dedication, and commitment to lead, train, and love your soldiers. You must want to command people more than anything else in the world.

YOU GOTTA HAVE THE BASICS: The basics include integrity, courage, loyalty, humility, and respect. You either have these basics or you don't. If they aren't a part of you now, unfortunately, they probably never will be. Simply said, these basics are the givens that must be practiced automatically. Violate a "given" you've set up for your troops and you're doomed to fail.

YOU GOTTA HAVE COURAGE: The basic of courage is so important that it deserves separate treatment. Call it "guts," "intestinal fortitude," "risk-taking," "bravery"—whatever: You must have this quality. As the commander, you're responsible for everything that happens. If you think an action is wrong, stand up and tell your soldiers what you think. Your opinion may not always satisfy the troops, but you'll establish a reputation as a commander whom they know looks out for his or her unit. But, be smart when you take this stand. Pick the right times, the right places, and the right issues.

YOU GOTTA BE FAIR: If you are fair in everything you do, everything else will fall into place. Being fair is treating *every* soldier even-handedly and with individual dignity and respect. How can you discipline a private first class for violating the company smoking policy, if your operations sergeant does it every day? How can you put a sergeant on the remedial PT program for consistently failing his physical fitness test, if one of your platoon leaders can't pass a physical fitness test? If you set double standards, you'll quickly undermine your soldiers' trust and willingness to follow your example. *A substitute for fairness doesn't exist.*

YOU GOTTA LEAD BY EXAMPLE: The most important attribute for success is leading by example. If you lead by example in everything you do, you'll succeed. Be a second-to-none role model to your officers, NCOs, and soldiers. They'll willingly follow a leader who lives both a "do as I say" *and* "do as I do" attitude.

War Story

A battalion commander felt so strongly about leading by example, he developed a "Follow-the-Leader Day." Every NCO and officer in the battalion had to complete this day of instruction, led personally *by the battalion commander and his CSM.*

The commander's intent was to develop the belief that **LEADERS ARE STANDARD-BEARERS** *and, as such, have no excuse not to lead by example in everything they do or say. Therefore, he conducted this training in the open, so all young enlisted soldiers could see what leading by example was all about. The day went like this:*

- *PT—Rigorous, varied, and instructional; for example, three kinds of push-ups and sit-ups, topped off by a four- mile group run.*
- *In-ranks inspection—From head-to-toe and front-to-rear. The battalion commander inspected the officers, and the CSM inspected the NCOs.*
- *Room standards—Participants visited three different rooms to see what a soldier's room should look like when he's on duty, when he's off duty, and for an official inspection.*
- *Lunch—A group lunch in the dining facility.*
- *Teach/coach time—Lecture and discussion on leadership, safety, and security.*
- *Rap session—Until now, it was a one-way street and the commander was driving. Now, after seven or eight hours in the front seat, he took a back seat and listened, and responded to any subject raised by participants.*

Follow-the-Leader Day helped officers and NCOs see they had to lead by example, even in "basic" behavior—including their own.

YOU GOTTA CARE: The "gut-most" important point is you have to care for your company and your troops! You must be sincere and willing to go that extra mile for your soldiers. Soldiers can distinguish a "ticket-punching," insincere commander from one who wants to command for all the *right* reasons. Only grudgingly do they follow a commander who's just going through the motions of command.

War Story

An experienced company commander overheard her first sergeant helping a soldier go on emergency leave because of a death in the family. Because the soldier needed money and had to leave immediately, the company commander personally intervened with the Red Cross to obtain a $200 loan for her soldier. The first sergeant drove the soldier to the bank, then to the airport.

The soldier returned 10 days later, and repaid the Red Cross his next payday. The soldier never forgot the concern shown by his commander and his first sergeant. Word spread throughout the company that both cared for their soldiers.

YOU GOTTA HAVE CONFIDENCE: If you don't believe in yourself, nobody else will. If you are decisive and show your troops you are eager to solve their problems, the confidence will be contagious.

YOU GOTTA BE ORGANIZED: A company commander has more to do than he or she can ever personally accomplish. Here are two keys to being organized: Managing time and delegating tasks.

Time is your most precious asset; use it wisely to organize yourself. Share the workload by delegation. It strengthens your chain of command by demonstrating confidence in your subordinate leaders. Once you delegate, give your subordinates a chance to do their jobs. They know their jobs better than you do.

Here's a checklist, drawn from many management experts, that will help you stay organized. Look it over and see what applies to you. Then make your own list. Keep this list around and look at it at least once a month. You'll be *amazed* at how much it will help you stay organized.

GOALS:

–Rewrite your goals once a month.

–Put signs in your office to remind you of goals.

DECISIONMAKING:

–Know when to say "no."

–Know when to stop a task.

–Know when to avoid involving unnecessary people in the decisionmaking process.

YOUR TIME:

–Continually ask yourself, "What is the best use of my time right now?"

–Set aside large chunks of time for tasks requiring uninterrupted concentration.

–Relax frequently and smile at the decision you've just made.

–Reward yourself when you've done important things.

ORGANIZE YOUR DAILY WORK:

–Keep a calendar of specific items to be done each day.

–Work on your "Things You'd Really Like to Do" list.

–Do your thinking on paper. Carry 3x5 cards. Write things down.

–Keep your desk top cleared; put the most important things in the center of your desk.

–Get rid of busywork; it's not how much you're *doing* that's important, but how much you get *done*.

–Throw away things you don't need.

–Ask yourself what you're avoiding when you're procrastinating.

MEETINGS:
   –Have a purpose when you hold a meeting, set a time
   limit, and ask only necessary individuals to take
   part.
   –Schedule meetings for a time just before lunch or
   quitting time; but realize that people have to be on
   their way—just like you do.
   –Try *stand-up* meetings; they tend to be brief and
   businesslike.
   –Ask open-ended questions. Listen actively.
CORRESPONDENCE:
   –Generate as little paperwork as possible.
   –Handle correspondence only once; trust your sig-
   nature at the bottom of the letter.
   –Write short letters and memos whenever you can.
   Otherwise, use the telephone.
   –Use simple charts or diagrams, rather than long,
   drawn- out papers, to communicate ideas.

YOU GOTTA ESTABLISH STANDARDS: Standards are
the foundation of your unit. Be tough and fair, but be reasonable. Involve your chain of command when developing company policy, because you want your standards to be their
standards and the unit's standards. If they understand your
standards, enforcing them will be easy. It's always better to
set *firm* standards when you *take over* a company, then ease
back, rather than to start out soft and try to get tough later.
The first way earns you respect; the second will earn you a
weak reputation. Whatever you do, don't ignore the standards you set, because when you do, you set new and lower
ones.

★ ★ ★ ★ ★ *THE BRASS SAYS*

General Carl Vuono on standards: Draw on the past; be responsible for the present; and shape the future.

YOU GOTTA BE COMPETENT: Technical and tactical
proficiency are musts. Your soldiers look to you for answers

and solutions. You must produce. Read, study, and think your job, and you'll produce results. Consult with senior commanders when you're up against a tough problem.

★ ★ ★ ★ ★ *THE BRASS SAYS*

General John Pershing on competency: A competent leader can get efficient service from poor troops while, on the contrary, an incapable leader can demoralize the best of troops.

YOU GOTTA BE YOURSELF: Being yourself got you where you are today. You know yourself better than anyone else. When you become a company commander, don't be awed by the power of your new position and change your personality. It won't work. There was only one Eisenhower and one Patton. Just like there's only one *you*.

YOU GOTTA MAKE THINGS HAPPEN: Be a doer. Get involved and be seen. Develop a reputation for making important things happen in your unit. But know when to get involved and when to let your chain of command handle problems. Act; never react.

YOU GOTTA DEVELOP TEAMWORK: Teamwork builds unit cohesiveness, that necessary bond that must exist among soldiers. No one has won a war by himself, lately.

Tip The Army, and commanders in general, are fairly good at rewarding individuals for their accomplishments. But when was the last time a squad or platoon in your unit was recognized *as a unit* for an accomplishment? Group recognition solidifies the importance of teamwork.

YOU GOTTA CHECK, CHECK, AND RECHECK: Because you, as company commander, direct that something be done doesn't always mean it will be done. Keep checking until your subordinates consider it business as usual. *Remember, that which is not inspected is neglected.*

YOU GOTTA BE AN ACTIVE LISTENER: As a general rule, you, as well as other company commanders, must work at developing the quality of being an active listener. If you act before hearing all the input, you'll make mistakes. Active listening means keeping your mind from wandering off to tomorrow's inspection; maintaining eye-to-eye contact with the speaker; asking for clarification when necessary; and providing the speaker feedback to ensure that you heard what he intended you to hear. It's easier to make decisions once you've heard the entire story.

★ ★ ★ ★ ★ *THE BRASS SAYS*

Colonel Mike Malone on listening: *Listen* to what your subordinates have to say to you. Take a few notes. In many cases, this is good feedback for you from the men who are on the receiving end of your leadership. *Listen* and learn.

Always give everyone his or her day in court. If your operations NCO proposes a change in procedures, don't make a snap decision. First, let him present his entire proposal. Then, if you **Tip** disagree, tell him no and the *reasons* why. Your chain of command must feel free to present new ideas without fear of immediate rejection. Only then do you inspire creative thinking and innovation. When you buy a subordinate's idea, recognize that person for it, especially when you're complimented on its success.

YOU GOTTA HAVE COMPASSION: Compassion is absolutely essential for a leader. Compassion doesn't mean you're weak. It means you're sympathetic—fair—to your soldiers when you should be. Command is tough, and you gotta be tough, but you can't be unmoved by your soldiers' problems.

★ ★ ★ ★ ★ *THE BRASS SAYS*

General Omar Bradley on compassion: Far from being a handicap to command, compassion is the measure of it. For unless one values the lives of his soldiers and is tormented by their ordeals, he is unfit to command.

YOU GOTTA KNOW YOUR BOSS: Some new company commanders get carried away with their own agenda and forget that boss-imposed tasks must go to the top of the priority list:

- Know your boss's idiosyncrasies. You've got some, so don't be surprised to learn that the boss has them too.
- Keep your boss informed. Like you, he doesn't welcome surprises. *Remember, bad news gets worse with age.* Better he should hear bad news from you . . . than from his boss.
- Be totally honest with your boss. He must be able to trust your word.
- If in doubt, seek your boss's counsel. This axiom is not a sign of weakness—it's smart business. It also tells him you're not a know-it-all and you'll also get the benefit of his experience.

YOU GOTTA BE FLEXIBLE: If you can't roll with the punches and be flexible, you're in trouble. Don't box yourself into a corner by not having a "plan B"—such as one for inclement weather.

YOU GOTTA BE PRACTICAL: Sometimes the quality of being practical is lost in the heat of the moment. Commanders must think first, be cool under pressure, and use common sense. New commanders tend to go "by the book" in the early stages. That's okay, but if the situation dictates a change, don't be afraid to make your move. A good sense of humor helps reduce stress and maintain stability in a unit. It places the demands and pressures of commanding a company into a proper perspective.

YOU GOTTA BE A SALESMAN: If *you* don't sell your unit, nobody will. You're your unit's commander *and* its public relations director. Let your unit's actions speak louder than words.

Tip Invite your boss and his command sergeant major to take part in some meaningful training or be present at a soldier's award ceremony. Seize the upper hand; it could help you avoid their unannounced visits. Surprise visits tend to be less than pleasant occasions.

YOU GOTTA HAVE FUN: Having fun and being a company commander are not contradictory. Commanding a *successful* company is like managing a *winning* baseball team—it's fun! Encourage your soldiers to take leave, and take it yourself.

Your Actions Prior to Command

THINK: A common problem for company grade officers going into command is that they don't take time to think how they want to command. They don't develop a vision of where they want their company to go. The most important step is to develop that mental road map and then commit it to writing.

Sit back and reflect on the direction you want to take a company *before* you actually take command. Once you assume command, 1,000 alligators will threaten to bite your butt every day while you're trying to drain the swamp.

Isolate yourself for at least an hour every other day for 10 days and think, read, and contemplate on the nature of command. If you really want a command, you'll think about your actions as a future commander several years before you command. You'll watch and learn from your current company commander the right and wrong ways to do things. Once you receive the guidon, you'll have a "honeymoon" of about 60 seconds . . . and then your battalion commander will expect you to be off and running. You better know where you are going.

EDUCATE YOURSELF: Talk with individuals and visit key organizations *before* your change of command.

Talk with key individuals:
- Your fellow company commanders.
- Your future executive officer and battalion command sergeant major.
- Several commanders who recently relinquished command.
- One senior officer whose thoughts and ideas you value.

Ask questions, such as these:
- What was your vision before taking command?
- How did you prepare to take command?
- Do you have any documents I can read to help me prepare?
- What will the battalion commander expect of me in the first 90 days?
- What are the strengths and weaknesses of the unit I'm about to command?
- What did you do the first week of your command?
- If you had to do it all over again, what would you do differently?

Visit key organizations:
- The inspector general's office.
- The provost marshal's office.
- The judge advocate general's office.
- The Material Assistance Inspection Team (MAIT).
- Your battalion and brigade staff principals.

Ask questions, such as these:
- What policies are causing company commanders problems?
- What assistance can I expect from you? Does your organization provide assistance visits?
- What regulations should I know best?
- Which companies do you like best—and why?

Your goal is to educate yourself by visiting and talking with as many people as possible. Evaluate their input and *THINK* how you want to incorporate other ideas into *your* game plan.

SPEND TIME WITH THE OUTGOING COM-MANDER: Spend as much transition time as possible with the outgoing commander. Get his or her views on the unit's strengths and weaknesses. Ask about any "unfinished business."

Have the outgoing commander give you a status report on where the unit is today in all areas, such as training, supply, and maintenance. Know what's been done, so you don't waste time.

A word of caution: You can spend too much time with the outgoing commander. Since this command probably is your first, you'll think you need more transition time than necessary. You may be new, but the vast majority in your subordinate chain of command is not. They're capable of answering your questions, are anxious to brief and help you, and may view too much time with the outgoing commander as a "negative." Open your mind as well as your door to your subordinates.

★ ★ ★ ★ ★ *THE BRASS SAYS*

Major General Perry Smith on taking over: One of the first things a new leader might do is ask the present leader to make a tape recording outlining major issues, concerns, problems, and frustrations that have occurred in the organization. . . . Additionally, the incumbent should outline in that tape any "skeletons in the closet" that exist in the organization so the new leader can be sensitive to issues and problems that might not be visible during the crucial first few months.

DRAFT YOUR COMMAND PHILOSOPHY: Prepare your command philosophy in *final draft* as soon as you've had time to read, talk with key individuals, and think about what you want to do.

One of the keys to being a successful company commander is to be yourself. More than any other document, your command philosophy should express your personal beliefs about how you want to command the unit. Content and format are your options. Some commanders develop lengthy documents to cover almost every subject in the unit. Others have shorter command philosophies, focused more on their leadership style.

A lengthy command philosophy could include the following:

>   –Duty environment (duty hours, time off, and leave).
>   –Leadership philosophy (decisionmaking, supervision).
>   –Unit standards.
>   –Training.
>   –Maintenance.
>   –Physical training.
>   –Drugs and alcohol.
>   –Safety.
>   –Discipline.
>   –Pride and esprit-de-corps.
>   –Security awareness.
>   –Uniform appearance.
>   –Education.
>   –Reenlistment.
>   –Readiness.
>   –Awards.
>   –Reports, correspondence, and suspenses.
>   –Communication.
>   –VIP visits.
>   –Quality of life.

A shorter leadership statement can include your philosophy as a commander:

>   –Memories fail; always write down ideas.
>   –When I ask for your opinion, I want to hear your opinion, not what you think I want to hear.

–Be aggressive and responsible. Never try to transfer blame to another—it destroys your credibility. If you step on it, admit it; then fix it.

–Don't bring me a problem, unless you have at least one recommended solution. Be a problem solver—not a problem maker or messenger.

–I'm very straightforward. That statement means at times you may hear things you don't like. But one thing for sure—you'll know where I stand. I'll be honest with you, and I expect you to be honest with me.

–*I* don't micro-manage or over-supervise—don't you do it either.

–This unit is a winner, not a loser. Here are my differences between winners and losers:

> The Winner is part of the answer.
> The Loser is part of the problem.

> The Winner has a program.
> The Loser has an excuse.

> The Winner says, "Let me help you do it."
> The Loser says, "That's not my job."

> The Winner sees an answer in every problem.
> The Loser sees a problem in every answer.

> The Winner says, "It may be difficult but we can do it."
> The Loser says, "It may be possible but it's too difficult."

> The Winner sees something wrong and fixes it on the spot.
> The Loser sees something wrong and procrastinates.

A command philosophy lets your subordinates understand their new commander—her intent, purpose, and direction. The thoughts in your command philosophy don't have to be original: After all, you aren't the first captain to ever command. Get a copy of your battalion commander's command philosophy, so you'll know his direction. Read it; then draft your own.

On assuming command and *after* you've listened to your soldiers, finalize your command philosophy. By waiting awhile, you give yourself time to adjust your ideas, based on your observations of the unit. Once you're satisfied with your philosophy, print it, and distribute it—*to every soldier in the unit.* Also ensure your boss, his CSM, and every newly arriving soldier receives a copy.

First Days and Weeks in Command

First impressions last the longest. When you take command, your soldiers will watch every move you make. They'll observe your appearance and note how you make decisions. You don't get three strikes before you're out. Just as you size up a new soldier when he reports to your unit, your soldiers are sizing you up.

At the same time, you get a first impression of the unit. Look at your unit as a new soldier would. Ask yourself these questions:

- Is the outside area attractive, suggesting a proud company?
- Is the inside of the unit clean and ready for an unannounced VIP visit?
- Is military courtesy routine?
- Are unit formations conducted according to FM 22-5, *Drill and Ceremonies*?
- Are the billets' standards high?
- Do my soldiers present a good military appearance?
- After two days in the unit, would a soldier feel he is in a unit that cares?

Your new soldiers also are looking at you. Their impressions—good or bad—get laid at your feet, even if you're the new kid in town. It "ain't fair" . . . but that's the way it is, because you're the commander.

Here are some dos and don'ts to consider during your first weeks in command:

DOs

OBSERVE AND LISTEN: If your unit ever needs a good listener, it's now. Keep your eyes open and watch how the unit goes about its daily business. Ask questions. Let everyone give you his or her opinion on the state of the unit. Be a sponge and soak it up.

HAVE PATIENCE: Don't try to change things overnight. If the unit is really as bad as some people tell you, your predecessor would have been relieved. Command is a new experience for you; take your time.

CHECK YOUR SUBORDINATES: Test the abilities of your subordinates. Give them challenging tasks and check their proficiency and responsiveness. You'll quickly distinguish your leaders from those who need your special kind of motivation.

BE FIRM RATHER THAN EASY: It's better to demand more in the beginning and then ease up, than to be too lenient and try to tighten the screws later. Above all, be yourself.

DO A UNIT CLIMATE PROFILE: DA Pam 600-69, *Unit Climate Profile*, spells out how to administer a unit climate profile analysis. Read this pamphlet thoroughly and give the survey to your unit to determine climate factors, such as cohesiveness, morale, attitude toward training, and living and working conditions. Do the profile by platoons. Although you may find significant differences between platoons, don't use the survey to compare them. The personality of the leadership is different and can affect the survey. Use the profile to improve *each* platoon and *your* unit in general. Use it to identify priorities for instituting new programs, or refocusing your soldiers' attention.

SURVEY YOUR SUBORDINATE LEADERSHIP: Ask your platoon sergeants, platoon leaders, section chiefs, and first sergeant to write out responses to the following questions:

- What does this unit do best?
- What does this unit do worst?
- What programs and policies should be stopped or changed? Why?
- What programs and policies should be continued without change? Why?
- If you were the new commander, what would you do differently?

Give your subordinates three days to complete the task. Their responses will tell you a lot about them and the pulse of the unit.

Tip

Written responses to questions give you a chance to see who can think and write. They help determine whether your officers and NCOs need certain professional development.

DEVELOP A FAMILY NEWSLETTER: Let your soldiers' spouses and families know you're the new commander and are concerned for their welfare. Let them know you're available to help them with their problems, and also give them a *general* idea of your expectations for the unit.

Tip

Mail the family newsletter directly to the spouse; it provides a more personal touch—and it gets there. You might consider a monthly spouse newsletter from you and your spouse. Open lines of communication with your soldiers' families is the crux.

DON'Ts

DON'T BE A KNOW-IT-ALL: Being a know-it-all is the quickest way to shut off communication. Instead, you want your soldiers to open up and tell you what they think.

DON'T MAKE QUICK CHANGES: Every unit fears that a new commander will make quick changes. As you observe and listen, you'll note things you want to change . . . to put your personal stamp on immediately. Don't. Tell your soldiers you do not make quick, arbitrary changes. Nothing is worse than a new commander who comes in and immediately changes established procedures, particularly if they were closely associated with a popular ex-commander. Tell them you'll change any situation that is dangerous or harmful to your soldiers or unit. Most changes, however, deserve your *thoughtful* and *careful* deliberation.

DON'T BAD MOUTH THE "OLD GUY": Your predecessor could be the biggest zero this side of the Mississippi—but don't bad mouth him. You're now the commander; if you want something changed, give the order and it will happen. Don't say, "This is all screwed up and shows total ignorance on Captain Smith's part and I'm changing it." This attitude will reduce your stature in the eyes of your subordinates.

DON'T BRAG: You've been selected to fill a very important position with more power than you ever thought possible. Don't let it go to your head.

Soldiers know you're good or you wouldn't be a company commander. Statements like "I'm going to make this rag bag unit a first–class outfit" will just turn your soldiers off. Remember the difference between confidence and bragging: Confident commanders don't brag—they get their unit to produce.

★ ★ ★ ★ ★ *THE BRASS SAYS*

Lieutenant General Julius W. Becton, Jr., on bragging: Remember, you have been appointed—not anointed!

After 90 Days the Unit Is Yours

Technically, the unit is yours from day one; however, the time will come when you can't blame the old commander for the problems in the unit. Around the 90-day mark, the reality will hit you that the unit, with all its warts, successes, and challenges, is now yours—lock, stock, and arms room.

Regulations require a courtesy inspection from your battalion commander within the first 90 days. Insist that the inspection be thorough—to find what's wrong so you can fix it. It's an excellent means of getting an independent view of your unit's strengths and weaknesses, and a chance to confirm your views. The results may cause you to change the unit's direction. Make necessary adjustments, but don't berate the supervisors of sections that did poorly. Your goal is to correct deficiencies. If one of your section supervisors can't cut the mustard, quickly replace him.

After your "free" inspection, write your boss a formal letter assessing strengths and weaknesses in the company and how you propose to fix the problems. Consider attaching this letter to your OER support form and use it as part of your goals and objectives. Don't be self-serving and exaggerate the weaknesses. Don't supply excuses and never, never, never use your "newness" to mitigate deficiencies. Simply state the facts and how you intend to fix the problems and capitalize on the ongoing good programs in the unit.

Tip

★ ★ ★ ★ ★ *THE BRASS SAYS*

General George C. Marshall on leading: The soldier is a man; he expects to be treated as an adult, not a schoolboy. He has rights; they must be made known to him and thereafter respected. He has ambition; it must be stirred. He has a belief in fair play; it must be honored. He has a need of comradeship; it must be supplied. He has imagination; it must be stimulated. He has a sense of personal dignity; it must be sustained. He has pride; it can be satisfied and made the bedrock of character once he has been assured that he is playing a useful and respected role. To give a man this is the acme of inspired leadership. He has become loyal because loyalty has been given to him.

The Bottom Line
for
Taking Command

- Company command is the most demanding job in the Army.

- Soldiers need leadership—don't disappoint them.

- Educate yourself and think *before* you take command.

- Make deliberate changes. Quick changes can be divisive for a unit.

- You "gotta" lead by example in everything you do.

- Publish *your* command philosophy. It's your unit's road map to success.

- Ensure you make a good first impression on your unit, and your unit makes a good first impression on new soldiers.

- Company command is the most rewarding job in the Army.

Bibliography for Taking Command

DA Pam 600-69, *Unit Climate Profile*.

FM 22-5, *Drill and Ceremonies*.

Malone, Dandridge M. *Small Unit Leadership*. San Francisco: Presidio Press, 1983.

Smith, Perry. *Taking Charge*. Washington, DC: National Defense University Press, 1986.

3. You and Your First Sergeant

No man is a leader until his appointment is ratified in the minds and hearts of his men.

Old Army Saying

THIS COULD HAPPEN TO YOU—It's your first opportunity to command a company. You've just assumed command of the worst unit in the battalion. In your initial interview with the battalion commander, he tells you your new unit has made a dramatic turnaround in the last six months, primarily because of the excellent work of a new first sergeant (1SG). Promoted the day he assumed his duties, the 1SG is smart and aggressive, leads by example, and has earned the respect of all the company's soldiers. He is the complete opposite of his "ROAD" (retired on active duty) predecessor, whom the battalion commander fired. The battalion commander directs you to maintain the good work your 1SG has started and to challenge your soldiers with meaningful training. In other words—don't screw up the first sergeant's good work. You're not a proven entity to your boss—your first sergeant is.

To your delight, you and your 1SG quickly develop a good working relationship. You listen. He teaches. You command the unit; he runs it. Although the two of you have differences of opinion, you communicate well and develop joint solutions. You also respect the fact that he's a family man with a very supportive wife and two boys. After four months, you and your boss couldn't be happier with the unit's progress.

At 0130 hours one morning you receive a telephone call from the military police station. The MPs ask you to pick up your 1SG, who has been charged with being drunk in public, disorderly conduct, and resisting apprehension. You can't believe it! When you arrive at the station, the MPs hand you a preliminary report. According to the report, your first sergeant went to the club for a quick beer with a few soldiers from your unit—something you knew he did occasionally.

In the past, he usually had only one beer, talked to the troops, and left. Last night, after many beers, he joined your soldiers in a brawl with soldiers from the unit next door. His right eye is black and blue, and he reeks with the smell of alcohol. Angry and disappointed, you sign for him and drive him to his quarters.

When you get home, you inform your battalion commander of the situation and tell him that you'll brief him on the circumstances and give him a recommendation after you've investigated the problem. He's less than overjoyed to receive the phone call.

When you arrive at your unit at 0630 hours, the first sergeant is waiting in your office. The unit already knows what's happened. What do you do now, Company Commander?

The Company Commander Commands the Unit; The First Sergeant Runs It

By now, you know you're responsible for everything that happens—or fails to happen—in your unit. However, that responsibility doesn't mean you have to do everything yourself. You have a strong right hand called a First Sergeant to help you and your unit.

As a *general* rule, the company commander **commands** the unit and the first sergeant **runs** it. But, this rule is a *general* rule and there's *overlap* in all areas. You can't do everything yourself; therefore, the Army has "issued" you an extra right hand with 17 to 23 years of experience to share part of the action. What action? That's for the two of you to work out between yourselves.

★ ★ ★ ★ ★ *THE BRASS SAYS*

Brigadier General John Johns on first sergeant responsibilities: The NCO support channel definitely needs more emphasis. The first sergeant should run the company and be the most knowledgeable soldier in it. By doing so, he gives the company commander *time* to lead the company.

On the other hand, don't be intimidated by his age and experience. How can you, a young captain in your twenties, tell someone with 21 years in the Army and six years of experience as a first sergeant, what to do? Remember, you have five to eight years of good experience in the Army yourself and it's your company. It's what you do *today* with whatever experience you happen to have that matters.

War Story

A parish priest asked an ROTC college senior to escort a retired Marine brigadier general to Mass on Sundays because the general was losing his eyesight and needed help. The student agreed and gradually he and the general became friendly. The general, in fact, enjoyed the student's persistent questions.

One Sunday after Mass and over breakfast, the soon-to-be commissioned "butter bar" asked the general a tough question. He was soon to be a platoon leader telling a platoon sergeant with 14 to 17 years of experience what to do. He worried about all the platoon sergeant's experience versus the four years of ROTC and a few summer camps that were all he had to draw on. How was he going to tell this platoon sergeant anything?

The old general sat back and laughed, and said that his answer not only applied to the relationship between a new lieutenant and a platoon sergeant but also to a new company commander and a veteran first sergeant. The answer was simple: "You pick out your good platoon sergeants and good first sergeants and listen and learn from them. Disregard what the bad platoon sergeants and first sergeants have to say."

"Sounds simple enough," the student replied, "but how do I tell the good ones from the bad ones?"

The general replied, "You'll easily distinguish the good from the bad. The good ones visit their soldiers at night and on the weekend. They ensure that every soldier eats and sleeps while in the field. They care to make it happen. Once you pick out the good platoon sergeants, you listen, learn, and reap the rewards."

*The general concluded with a final thought: **"Don't roll over. Remember, you're in charge, and the really good platoon sergeants and first sergeants train** their lieutenant or captain without him ever knowing it."*

Educate Yourself

TALK WITH YOUR FELLOW COMPANY COMMAND-ERS: Draw on their experience. They know your first sergeant's reputation in the battalion; they've had similar situations and can tell you how they're handling them. Ask their advice:

- What is essential in a good first sergeant?
- What is the first sergeant's role in Uniform Code of Military Justice (UCMJ) matters? In training?
- What are a first sergeant's biggest mistakes?
- How do I work out disagreements with my first sergeant?
- How does the battalion CSM handle the first sergeants?

- What do you know about my first sergeant that I don't?

Each company commander has a different opinion on the relationship between the company commander and a first sergeant. That's okay! Remember: Unit missions, personalities, and locations vary. Your goal is to better prepare for your own commander/first sergeant relationship.

TALK WITH THE FIRST SERGEANTS IN OTHER COMPANIES: Talking with someone else's first sergeant may seem strange, but every story has two sides: You want to see how other first sergeants view things. The ones you talk with will know and explain what a good first sergeant does. Ask them the same questions you asked their bosses. Keep the conversation on a professional, rather than a personal basis. Be direct and don't pull punches. Be sincere and *objective.* First sergeants, as a group, agree on one rule: **Good first sergeants make rookie captains good commanders.**

★ ★ ★ ★ ★ *THE BRASS SAYS*

SMA Julius W. Gates on company commanders: My job as a first sergeant was to make *my* company commander the best company commander in the battalion—period!

TALK WITH YOUR BATTALION CSM: Your battalion CSM probably has been a first sergeant several times and has trained many a company commander. He not only will explain what an ideal 1SG does, but should tell you the strengths and weaknesses of your current first sergeant and how you can help him or her. Develop a rapport with the battalion CSM to last throughout your command tour. If you're having problems with your 1SG, seek the battalion CSM's advice. Maybe your first sergeant's okay and *you're* doing something wrong.

TALK WITH YOUR BATTALION COMMANDER: You've formed thoughts concerning the proper relationship between a company commander and a first sergeant. Now, listen to your battalion commander's answers to pertinent questions. He'll tell you his opinion of your 1SG and give you guidance on your relationship. As your unit goes, so goes his battalion. Keep both the battalion commander and the command sergeant major informed of problems between you and your first sergeant.

Ideal Company Commander–First Sergeant Relationship

A productive company commander–first sergeant relationship is your goal because such a relationship means success for your unit. Mutual respect is essential. Think about these areas in building an excellent relationship:

COMMUNICATION: Communication must be **open, direct, and two-way.** The commander and the first sergeant must constantly tell each other what they do. If they talk, they'll speak with one voice. Tell your first sergeant that he or she will always be able to speak freely and openly. Military courtesy prevails, but remember—once you close the door to your office, expect candid discussions. Tell him or her that, although you probably won't accept *all* recommendations, you will always seek *and respect* open and direct advice.

Tip   Have a *short* session with your first sergeant at least once a day—in the morning or in the evening. Make these sessions a permanent part of your everyday calendar.

CONFIDENCE: In a solid company commander–first sergeant relationship, each has total confidence in the other's ability. Mutual **support** is essential: Your first sergeant must be certain of your support. A first sergeant not certain of the company commander's support is an indecisive leader. You achieve solid support only if that confidence has *mutual* **trust** and *two-way* **loyalty.** Of course, the company commander can never back bad decisions. *Blind* loyalty is poor leadership. If your first sergeant is wrong, say so. And expect similar frankness in return. Once you establish mutual support, trust, and loyalty, confidence in each other will follow.

COOPERATION AND TEAMWORK: Cooperation solidifies a good relationship. Neither of you should put the other in a win/lose situation: "I'm right or else." Each must admit mistakes and know when to give in. Commanding a company requires the teamwork of two knowledgeable, professional leaders. They're a team: Together they stand; divided they fall.

CLEAR GOALS AND REASONABLE STANDARDS: Immediate agreement on goals for the company is essential. Most soldiers will meet your expectations if they clearly understand them. Speak with one voice as you apply those standards: Firm but fair standards are best; impossibly demanding ones can only lead to failure. If you're uncertain at first, be hard. It's easier to *relax* high standards than to be too *lax*. Commanders who start tough and then ease up a bit gain respect; those who start soft at first and back down when trouble comes are seen by their troops as weak.

FRIENDSHIP: An ideal company commander–first sergeant relationship is essential. Friendship is not essential, but it sure makes life a lot easier. Friendship in this sense is not calling each other by a first name. Mutual esteem is more like it—the natural result of a relationship based on open communication and teamwork. Friendship means agonizing with your "right hand" over the tough decisions affecting the lives of your soldiers and their families.

Tip Invite your first sergeant and his or her family over for a backyard barbecue occasionally. Don't talk shop. Relax and have your families get to know each other. You strengthen your relationship with your 1SG when you get to know the "whole" person, not just the person at the office.

Common Problems

While an ideal company commander–first sergeant relationship is a goal, you can realistically expect problems between you and your first sergeant. Here are some of the more common problems:

LACK OF COMMUNICATION: If good communication is the greatest asset between a company commander and a first sergeant, bad communication can be the worst liability; so routine daily meetings where both speak freely are essential. Not keeping each other informed spells disaster.

YOU'RE BULLHEADED; THE 1SG HAS A DIFFERENT AGENDA: Many new company commanders are headstrong and self-assured. They tend to disregard the advice of their experienced and capable 1SG. A few blunders usually bring them back to reality, but you can avoid that humiliation with common sense. Listen to your first sergeant; draw on that long experience. Now, if your first sergeant is cocksure about what will and won't work and has no tolerance for something new, you've got just as big a problem as if you were bullheaded. A stubborn and rigid first sergeant has a fixed agenda: "This young, inexperienced captain had better 'get in step' in this unit." In this situation, you must take charge. Pity the poor company with both a bullheaded commander and an arrogant first sergeant. Shakespeare said of a similar situation: "Confusion now hath made its masterpiece." You must undo the confusion.

LACK OF AGREEMENT ON UNIT GOALS AND STANDARDS: First sergeants and COs should decide *jointly* on the direction for the unit. It's a problem easily solved. The company commander commands; the first sergeant takes direction and runs with it.

LACK OF MUTUAL SUPPORT AND RESPECT: The problem of lack of mutual support and respect usually doesn't happen overnight, but it can develop over time when the company commander and 1SG fail to communicate. Left unattended, lack of mutual support and respect can divide a unit.

PERSONALITY CONFLICTS: Personality conflicts should never disrupt an Army company. Seasoned commanders often say that a personality conflict in a senior-subordinate relationship can't exist—only a "communication problem exists." The best fix is to talk it out between the two of you. If necessary, seek advice from your battalion commander, battalion executive officer, or command sergeant major, but don't let it fester or it could harm your unit. Long-standing personality conflicts are the hardest to overcome.

What a First Sergeant Wants in a Commander

Meeting the expectations of a first sergeant isn't easy, especially if you're a rookie commander. But certain qualities will help you. Here's what any good first sergeant wants in a commander:

A CONFIDENT LEADER: The first sergeant doesn't need a fainthearted weakling at the helm. He or she wants a commander who **exudes** confidence in action, bearing, and thinking . . . one who leaves no doubt who's in charge. Remember, you must be a doer; get out from behind your desk and check training, maintenance, and your troops. It's better to be a decisive hardcharger who makes an occasional mistake than an indecisive *wimp* who doesn't.

AN OFFICER WHO LEADS BY EXAMPLE: Not the first time you've heard this saying, right? Lead by example in everything you do—**everything!**

Tip You know you're leading by poor example when your first sergeant comes into your office, shuts the door, and says, "Sir, we need to talk. You're inspecting the troops tomorrow afternoon and you need a haircut and your boots need shining." Your credibility just hit bottom. If he has to tell you something so basic, what kind of confidence will your subordinates have in your ability to command the unit?

A LEADER WHO CARES FOR HIS SOLDIERS: Your 1SG wants a commander who takes measures to respect, love, and protect his soldiers. You must be a commander who goes the extra mile because you're genuinely concerned for each soldier's welfare. This quality seems to develop (or fail to develop) early in life. You *can't* fake it.

A "COOL-HEADED" LEADER: Don't show your "hind end." Be mature and deal with difficult problems in a determined manner. Yellers and screamers are ineffective. A first sergeant wants a patient commander who employs common sense and uses practical application. Agree with your first sergeant to tackle your *most* difficult problems before other problems. Sometimes, just your determination to want the hard ones solved first breeds confidence. (And confident leaders have a way of getting lucky.)

A LEADER WHO TRUSTS HIS NCOs: Words do not accomplish this feat of trusting your noncommissioned officers—actions do. Show trust for your NCOs by giving mission-type orders to demonstrate their ability. Make your goals and standards clear, then let your NCOs *perform*. Don't clobber them the first time they make a mistake. Do it the second time.

A LEADER WHO'S A BUFFER: Be the buffer between the battalion staff and your unit. Filter out training detractors and unnecessary community details—but in a positive way: "We'd love to help with that project, but we're two days away from deploying to the field for a month. We were the only company on the entire post chosen for the task. When we return, let's get together, review the bidding, and maybe we can help then." In other words, keep the mission first and protect your people against the peripheral stuff and the "nice-ifs."

A LEADER WHO ADMITS MISTAKES: No one's infallible. With the power you have as a company commander, you may begin to *think* you're incapable of error, but you **will** make mistakes. Be big enough to admit you're wrong and learn from it. Then don't make the same mistake twice. **Admit mistakes to your troops: It will encourage honesty and candor in them!**

What a First Sergeant Doesn't Want in a Commander

A normal, healthy first sergeant "ain't bashful." He'll quickly tell you what qualities guarantee failure in a company commander. For example:

A COMMANDER WHO WON'T LISTEN: Your first sergeant wants and needs to be heard. First sergeants may not always be right, but their experience and position warrant your listening. You don't have to agree with every recommendation, but you *should* listen. A wise old commander once said: **"You have two ears and one mouth. If you have a *good* first sergeant, you ought to listen to him twice as much as you talk or tell him what to do."**

A COMMANDER WHO'S TOO AMBITIOUS: This commander accepts every task regardless: "Bring on the world. . . . We can handle it." His expectations of the unit are unrealistic and the resulting pressure on the unit causes low morale and inefficiency. The first sergeant says, "Sir, but . . . " and the commander replies, "Don't worry about it, first sergeant, we can handle it." Sound familiar? **Know when to say "No!"**

A COMMANDER WHO'S INDECISIVE: A commander who can't, or won't, make a decision keeps a unit in the cellar forever. A first sergeant usually can live with a mediocre decision more easily than with no decision at all. When you've considered the alternatives, the options, the "on-the-other-hands"—decide. Don't think out loud in front of your NCOs and soldiers. What they need from you are the magic words, "Okay, here's what we do."

A COMMANDER WHO WINGS IT: The commander who wings it acts first and thinks second. The unit has no direction and no standards because everything's spur-of-the-moment. If you tend to be that way, *force* yourself to hold planning sessions. Tell your first sergeant to schedule a planning meeting—say once a month; do nothing else but review your current situation and *plan* where you want to be by a specific time. Sometimes, a commander won't have time to plan but must decide based on the best available information at the time. As a *team*, you and your first sergeant can do it!

Tip

The pressure of the job and the demand for instant results can easily cause a company commander to react, instead of plan and act. If you tend to react instead of plan, tell the 1SG about your tendency and that you want advice. Planning on a regular basis often solves this problem and your 1SG can help.

A COMMANDER WHO MICROMANAGES: Micromanagement drives any first sergeant up a wall and it's especially tough on good first sergeants. A micromanaging commander doesn't know how to give a mission-type order. He sends an unfortunate signal to his subordinates: "I don't have confidence in you." Delegate and give mission-type orders. Your subordinates won't grow if you don't.

A COMMANDER WHO'S A DESK RIDER: A commander who is most comfortable at a desk will never survive. Paperwork and correspondence are important, but not at the expense of checking your soldiers. You can't know the "pulse" of your unit if you never leave your desk. Tell your first sergeant to feel free to remove you from your chair if necessary. And promise to *return* the favor: This desk-riding disease is contagious—first sergeants also can have it. Remember, paperwork can be done more quickly early or late in the day, with less interruptions.

What a Commander Wants in a First Sergeant

Expect the first sergeant to be the **best soldier in the unit**. You could describe the top soldier in these terms:

A STRONG LEADER: You want a first sergeant who's motivated—a person who takes charge. He should demonstrate confidence not only to you, but to the troops. He adjusts his leadership style depending on the situation: He knows when to "chew" and when to console.

A LEADER BY EXAMPLE: Just as a first sergeant wants a company commander to lead by example, you want your top soldier to do the same. A first sergeant who leads by example establishes high standards that are not just *enforceable,* but infectious to everyone in the unit.

A COMPETENT LEADER: You need a first sergeant who's technically and tactically proficient and a self-starter who gives you the best advice—in other words, a competent leader. You should count your blessings (and *not* be intimidated or jealous) if your first sergeant is widely respected as the expert, the most knowledgeable soldier in the company.

A TRAINER AND DEVELOPER: Training is the first priority for every NCO, and it's your first sergeant's bread and butter. He must set the *individual* training standard for every soldier in the unit. His standards determine how your soldiers develop and how they accomplish the mission.

A GOOD COMMUNICATOR: A company commander needs someone who can speak and write. Good communication also includes listening. He must be able to articulate to you both sides of a problem. He can't do that if he doesn't *hear* both sides.

A DEDICATED LEADER: A company commander wants a first sergeant who cares for soldiers 24 hours a day. **The job mandates total dedication—nothing less.**

Tip Observe your first sergeant to see how many times he comes in the unit at night and on weekends. A dedicated first sergeant will visit HIS unit frequently after duty hours. You'll know he's doing his job when you run into him in the unit after duty hours. (He'll also know you're doing yours.)

A LOYAL SUPPORTER: Loyalty is a two-way street. A single breech of loyalty can destroy a good relationship. You have the right to expect fierce and dedicated loyalty from your first sergeant, because that loyalty is fundamentally and foremost to you *as company commander*—not to you as an individual. Loyalty to you as an individual will take time, and may not ripen at all.

What a Commander Doesn't Want in a First Sergeant

You know what you *don't* want in a 1SG. You've been a platoon leader and, possibly, an executive officer. You've formed ideas of what you *don't* want in a first sergeant:

A FIRST SERGEANT WHO DOESN'T LISTEN: Some first sergeants have their own agenda and suffer from the dreaded tunnel-vision disease. Your 1SG may not be receptive to new ideas, but you're the decisionmaker. Be direct, honest, and confident. Help your 1SG understand he must *listen* to you as well as advise you.

A FIRST SERGEANT WHO DOESN'T KEEP HIS COMMANDER INFORMED: Yes, you'll both be busy, but never too busy to let each other know what's going on. Your division of the workload demands daily and frequent communication. Insist on it.

A FIRST SERGEANT WHO DOESN'T SUPPORT HIS COMMANDER: Statements such as, "The commander said. . . . I tried to talk him out of it, but he said. . . ." don't promote unity or teamwork. A commander and first sergeant must support each other. When they don't, one of them must leave. The same is true of your relationship with the battalion commander. Don't return from the battalion training meeting and say, "He said we'll do it this way." The correct response is, "Here's the new procedure we're using—period!"

A FIRST SERGEANT WHO DOESN'T LEAD BY EXAMPLE: How can you give a soldier extra PT to pass the PT test if no one has ever seen your first sergeant take it? How can you tell a soldier to shine his boots if your 1SG's boots always need a shine and he looks as if he slept in his uniform? Get rid of double standards.

A FIRST SERGEANT WHO DOESN'T TRAIN AND HOLD HIS NCOs ACCOUNTABLE: If the top enlisted soldier doesn't train and hold his NCOs accountable, you'll have a 1SG in name only. Luckily, a 1SG with this problem is the exception rather than the rule. A 1SG is 1SG only when he holds himself and his soldiers accountable.

A FIRST SERGEANT WHO'S A DESK RIDER: Most good first sergeants delegate appropriately, so they spend little time behind the desk—they don't want to be desk bound. If you have a desk jockey, assign projects that can't be done at a desk. If the problem continues, talk it out. One "heart-to-heart" is all it should take.

A FIRST SERGEANT WHO OVERRULES LIEUTEN-ANTS' DECISIONS: Some first sergeants forget lieutenants are inexperienced and make mistakes. However, good platoon sergeants and 1SGs traditionally help make inexperienced lieutenants good company commanders. If your lieutenants complain that the 1SG is overriding their decisions, resolve the problem. If you let this situation fester, your lieutenants may hesitate to surface problems.

Day One With Your First Sergeant

The most important meeting with your first sergeant is the first one immediately after you assume command. Here, the two of you will establish the plan to command and run the company. Having this meeting soon after the change of command sends a powerful signal to the unit on the importance of the commander/first sergeant relationship.

Give your 1SG a week's notice about the meeting. Explain your agenda and ask him to be ready to discuss what the company's goals should be and other matters you consider important. Schedule a firm time and permit no outside interruptions. Try to accomplish the following:

- **GET** the first sergeant's ideas on a command philosophy.
- **DEVELOP** and agree on unit goals, standards, and objectives:
  - Specify and publish them. (For example, a goal of 260 for everyone on the PT test.)
  - Agree on "the forbiddens: the catastrophic non-redeemables." (For example, safety, weapons and ammunition accountability, drugs, DWI, and AWOL.) You and your first sergeant must be on the same "priority frequency" to ensure fairness.
  - Show your 1SG a copy of your completed OER Support Form.
- **DISCUSS** your expectations of a 1SG.
- **SEEK** the 1SG's expectations of you.
- **EMPHASIZE** open, two-way communication. For example, guarantee the 1SG his "day in court."

- **DETERMINE** the 1SG's role in UCMJ and adminis-
  trative separation procedures. For example, the 1SG:
  —Advises and recommends.
  —Initiates.
  —Checks to ensure you have all details and sup-
    porting documents to make a fair and just
    decision.
  —Protects soldiers' rights.
  —Supervises any punishment imposed.

Tip

UCMJ actions present the greatest opportunity for disagreement between a company commander and a 1SG. Open and two-way communication is vital! Discuss in detail the statement *compassion is not a sin* with your first sergeant. This statement should help both of you in your approaches to UCMJ matters.

- **DETERMINE** the 1SG's role with company lieuten-
  ants. The first sergeant:
  —Advises.
  —Trains.
  —Assists.
  —Listens.
  —Doesn't dictate.

War Story

A young second lieutenant received a severe lecture from her company commander because her platoon failed a unit inspection. The commander knew the lieutenant had potential and wanted to make sure this miserable performance wasn't repeated. She told the lieutenant she'd reinspect the platoon the next week and that the platoon had better be ready. The commander and first sergeant discussed the situation later that day and the commander suggested the first sergeant do a little "special work." The first sergeant agreed with the company commander and followed up with a talk with the platoon sergeant. Two days before the reinspection, the first sergeant took the lieutenant to a quiet place. During their discussion, the wise NCO gave detailed guidance on things the lieutenant should ensure were corrected and tips on how to "dazzle the company commander with her brilliance." The lieutenant was grateful and took the first sergeant's advice. (On the side, the first sergeant gave "firm" advice to the platoon sergeant also.) Fortunately, the second inspection went extremely well and the company commander heaped praise on the lieutenant, the platoon sergeant, and the troops. "I knew you all had it in you. . . ." On the way back to the office, the company commander smiled and said to her top soldier, "Keep up the good work, First Sergeant."

- **DETERMINE** a general division of labor. You should have a division of labor because you can't do everything yourself. You and your 1SG must agree on what areas each will emphasize and then keep each other *totally* informed. **You are responsible for what goes on in the unit**; however, you can better accomplish the mission if you and your 1SG share the workload. Here are some possibilities:

COMPANY COMMANDER:
  –Commands, plans, establishes policy, and allocates resources.
  –Outlines unit operations, readiness, and effectiveness.
  –Organizes collective training.
  –Promotes officer professional development.
  –Handles major disciplinary matters.

FIRST SERGEANT:
  –Conducts daily business, including health and welfare and quality-of-life matters.
  –Handles individual soldiers and their equipment, and team leading.

45

—Organizes individual training.
—Promotes NCO professional development.
—Handles minor disciplinary matters.

Considerable overlap exists, but don't totally shrug off your supervisor's duties in the 1SG's column.

• **DISCUSS** the "good-guy/bad-guy" role. Not everyone agrees there should be a good-guy/bad-guy role in a unit. The "book solution" says both the company commander and the 1SG need to be "good" or "bad," depending on the situation. Normally, the personalities of the company commander and the first sergeant determine roles. The 1SG, by the nature of the job and historical "mystique," is more often the "bad guy"; the company commander becomes the "good guy" because he or she lacks experience. **The true solution is to be yourself.** You and your 1SG should both be able to be tough or compassionate, as necessary.

A Bad First Sergeant

Ninety-nine times out of a hundred you will have a dedicated, capable 1SG. What about that one 1SG who is hopelessly ineffective? An inefficient 1SG can destroy a unit. He has to go and you have to make it happen.

Too often, company commanders are reluctant to relieve a 1SG because his or her career may be ruined. As a result, a nonproductive 1SG becomes a figurehead and a platoon sergeant becomes a de facto first sergeant. Obviously, everyone loses. The unit 1SG position is too important not to have the very best soldier for the job. Relieving your 1SG for inefficiency may well be the hardest thing you do in command. Such action should be taken only as a last resort. Do not confuse relief for inefficiency with relief for misconduct or crime. Consult your lawyer for procedures to follow when you have evidence of a crime or other misconduct. Consider these actions when relieving a 1SG for inefficiency:

• Review local regulations and directives. Senior commanders frequently specify procedures for relief of a senior NCO.

- Seek advice from your battalion commander and CSM. Inform them immediately of significant problems with your 1SG.
- Confront your 1SG verbally and in writing about your concerns.
- Give the 1SG assistance and support in correcting the problem.
- Allow sufficient time to correct the problem.
- As a last straw—write a 30-day-notice letter. This letter is official notification that the 1SG has 30 days to change or be relieved. Have your lawyer and battalion commander review the letter.
- Relieve your 1SG at the end of 30 days if he has not improved. Write a relief NCO-ER. Offer assistance in the reassignment process.

Two key points to remember in this situation: *One*, soldiers deserve the best leadership possible and your 1SG has to be **the** best leader; *two*, 1SG relief is a **"career-ender."**

Let's go back to the beginning for a moment . . .

Remember the drinking problem with your first sergeant and the fight in the club?
- Was it wrong for the first sergeant to go to the club occasionally and have *a* beer with the troops?
- What did he do wrong on the night in question?
- What does this incident do for his reputation in the eyes of his soldiers?
- As a result of this one incident, have you lost confidence in your first sergeant?
- Can he remain in his current position?
- What actions will you recommend to the battalion commander?

Answer these questions in light of what you've read in this chapter. If you don't know the answers to these questions, you should know where to find them.

The Bottom Line
for
You and Your First Sergeant

- The company commander **commands** the unit. The first sergeant **runs** the unit.

- Good first sergeants make rookie captains good commanders.

- Communication (open and two-way) is essential for a company commander—first sergeant relationship.

- Meet with your first sergeant on the *first* day. Discuss and resolve goals, standards, and roles.

- Problems between a commander and his top soldier, left unresolved, will destroy a unit.

- A first sergeant wants a company commander who leads by example in everything.

- A first sergeant doesn't want a company commander who is indecisive, overreacts, and doesn't plan.

- A company commander wants a first sergeant who's the best soldier in the unit.

- A company commander doesn't want a first sergeant who isn't a team player.

- An old, wise first sergeant once stated: "If you screw up, I screw up . . . and I don't screw up!"

4. Military Justice and Administrative Law Matters

Discipline must be a habit so ingrained that it is stronger
than the excitement of battle or the fear of death.

General George S. Patton, Jr.

THIS COULD HAPPEN TO YOU—A Sergeant First Class
assigned to your company in Southern Germany
has 16 years in the service and two years in his present rank.
After a review of his records, an interview, and your first sergeant's recommendation, you make him a platoon sergeant.
His family has deferred travel and won't arrive for several
months. This new platoon sergeant soon begins drinking
heavily after duty hours and acting erratically on duty—randomly praising some soldiers and reprimanding others. You
notice the soldiers reprimanded are usually female.

One night the platoon sergeant gets drunk at the NCO
club and then, on his way back to his temporary room in the
barracks, accosts a young female soldier from his unit. He
tries to convince her to come to his room. When she de-
clines, he pins her against the wall of a building, tells her
how beautiful she is, confesses he would like to become her
bed partner, and kisses her neck. Recognizing his inebriated
state, she placates him, steers him to his room, shoves him
in, closes the door, and runs to the CQ for help. When you
and your first sergeant learn of the situation the next morning, you inform the battalion commander. He orders an informal AR 15-6 investigation to determine the facts and to

afford the platoon sergeant a chance to respond to the allegations.

You conduct the AR 15-6 investigation, which not only substantiates the allegations but also reveals three similar incidents involving the platoon sergeant and other female soldiers. During each of these situations, the platoon sergeant was highly intoxicated. When asked why they didn't bring these incidents to the attention of the chain of command earlier, each of the female soldiers responds, "Who would believe my word over a sergeant first class? Besides, the chain of command wouldn't do anything about it anyway." Furthermore, you discover the platoon sergeant recently received an Article 15 for a similar offense at his last unit and was relieved from his job. This information wasn't in his Military Personnel Record Jacket, which he personally carried to your company on his transfer. When you question your platoon sergeant about the incidents, he refuses to make a statement.

What actions should you take? How should you discipline him? What organizations can help you make your decisions? Should you talk to all the female soldiers in your unit to see if general problems of this nature exist? These are just a few of the many questions you'll have to answer as a commander when you encounter similar situations. The decisions you make will send a message to your company. Before making such decisions, you should understand three matters: Your role, responsibility, and authority in the military justice system; the law and options available when you deal with violations of the Uniform Code of Military Justice (UCMJ); and the long- and short-term effects of your decisions on the unit you command.

The Company Commander's Judicial Responsibilities

You have two major responsibilities in the military justice arena: To enforce the law, and to protect the constitutional and UCMJ rights of all the soldiers you command.

ENFORCE THE LAW: The company commander ensures his troops understand and follow the UCMJ and all rules and regulations. You must base the standards of discipline for your unit on military laws and regulations. Your command philosophy letter to your troops already should contain your broadly stated idea about the most common violations. Everyone should already know your policies on such issues as alcohol and drug consumption, sexual harassment, and safety. In fact, it's a good idea to formulate unit standing operating procedures based on the UCMJ, battalion guidelines, Army practice, and your own good sense. Your lawyer can help you shape your SOPs.

PROTECT YOUR SOLDIERS' RIGHTS: Many company commanders, adept at enforcing the law, inadvertently violate the rights of soldiers. In the leadership example that opened this chapter, the sergeant first class obviously has to be punished for his offenses. But you also are responsible for ensuring that his rights are protected and that he receives legal counsel. Have your first sergeant schedule the legal appointment and make sure the platoon sergeant goes. Remember, your judicial responsibility is to make sure your soldiers are apprised of their legal rights.

The two goals of the military justice system are:
(1) Be fair to the individual.
(2) Make sure your policies reflect good discipline and order for the unit.

Educate Yourself

TALK WITH YOUR LAWYER: The most important thing you can do for yourself, your soldiers, your unit, your battalion commander, and the Army is consult your lawyer before taking **ANY** military justice action. Most organizations have a legal office with a young Judge Advocate whose responsibility is to advise you on military justice and administrative matters. In fact, meet your lawyer before you take command. He'll answer your questions and give you an opinion of the military justice system. It helps to develop a rapport that will last throughout your command. Cover everything from letters of reprimand to courts-martial, from search-and-seizure to administrative elimination proceedings. Don't leave his office until you're satisfied you can do your duty—legally. Make it a habit to confer with the Judge Advocate before taking action against a soldier or before publishing a policy.

Tip Many Judge Advocates also have handbooks or published guidelines with information for your particular convening authority's jurisdiction. Seek out this information. It will save you time and energy, and possibly prevent costly mistakes. A particularly good reference is FM 27-1, *Legal Guide for Commanders*. Use it.

TALK WITH YOUR BATTALION COMMANDER: You must understand your commander's philosophy on administering military justice. Before you leave his office, make sure you understand his policies on nonjudicial and nonpunitive measures, drugs, alcohol, leadership—EVERYTHING. You want to know if he personally reserves the right to exercise Article 15 authority over a particular case, or certain categories of offenders, or offenses. Best you find out how much he'll handle and how much he'll let you handle—before you have your first incident.

Discuss his Article 15 procedures and how he's handled certain offenders in the past. Your battalion commander most likely has been in your shoes several times. Draw on his experiences before you have to act on a difficult matter. First, learn all the facts, consult your lawyer for legal advice, develop your plan, then present it to your battalion commander for his advice. He may elect to handle the matter at his level or he may delegate the matter to you. However, he may not direct you any further.

Once the battalion commander delegates a matter to you, you must exercise your discretion to determine the appropriate action. After awhile you won't need to discuss routine matters. Your battalion commander will be confident in you and delegate increasing responsibility to you.

TALK WITH YOUR SUBORDINATE CHAIN OF COMMAND: Consult platoon leaders and platoon sergeants before acting against one of their soldiers. They know the soldier better than you and understand how the particular situation affects the platoon. But they also are close to their soldiers and could be too protective and could attempt to minimize the significance of an incident. The Army pays you and your first sergeant to recognize lack of objectivity. Over time, platoon leaders and sergeants will learn that you want *facts* to make informed decisions.

TALK WITH YOUR FIRST SERGEANT: Your first sergeant's experience is invaluable, and first sergeants have a way of getting to the heart of the matter. Make sure your first sergeant is present when you talk with platoon leaders and their platoon sergeants. Demonstrate your respect for him and solicit his advice—you're a team.

Know Your Options

As a company commander, you have a wide range of options for handling misconduct. As you'll quickly learn, a few problem soldiers will consume an inordinate amount of your time. Time is the one thing you will never be "issued" enough of. Try to reform the offending soldiers, but if your initial attempts fail, then consider elevating the level of disciplinary action. Generally, you'll want to dispose of an action at the lowest level commensurate with discipline and the nature of the offense and offender. Your options are administrative, nonjudicial, and judicial. Always identify your objectives when considering which option to take. For example, will an administrative measure correct a deficiency? If a soldier is found guilty of an offense, do you want to punish, rehabilitate, or eliminate him or her, or a combination of the three? Once you determine your objectives, choosing the appropriate option is easier.

ADMINISTRATIVE OPTIONS:

Administrative options run the gamut from nonpunitive measures to separation from the Army. Except for separation proceedings under AR 635-200, *Personnel*

Separations—Enlisted Personnel, administrative options generally teach proper standards of military conduct. Administrative options include the following:

- **Rehabilitative Measures**:
    - –Counseling (oral and written)
    - –Extra Training
    - –Admonitions
    - –Reprimands
    - –Rehabilitative Transfers
    - –Bars to Reenlistment
- **Loss of Discretionary Benefits**:
    - –Denial of Pass Privileges
    - –Denial of Allowance for Quarters
    - –Denial of Separate Rations
    - –Suspension of Driving License/Privileges
    - –Termination of Family Quarters
    - –Termination of Off-Duty Employment
    - –Bar to Entry on Installations
- **Adverse Administrative Actions Short of Separation**:
    - –Relief for Cause
    - –Removal from Promotion List
    - –Administrative Reduction in Grade
    - –Poor Evaluation Report
    - –Suspension of Security Clearance
    - –MOS Reclassification
- **Separation from the Military**:
    - –Alcohol and Drug Abuse
    - –Unsatisfactory Performance
    - –Overweight Problem
    - –Homosexuality
    - –Civil Conviction
    - –Acts or Patterns of Misconduct
    - –Personality Disorder
    - –Erroneous Enlistment
    - –Discharge for the Good of the Service

Even this long list isn't complete; so it's a solid idea to consult *your* lawyer before taking any final action.

Consider imposing rehabilitative measures and loss of discretionary benefits primarily for minor misconduct, particularly early on. These measures try to help an individual "soldier his way back" from a mistake. Let's review these administrative options, stressing first the rehabilitative measures.

Rehabilitative Measures

COUNSELING may be oral or written. Counseling for minor misconduct and substandard performance is a corrective and educational method. You inform a soldier why his or her performance is unacceptable, give notice that repeated or similar incidents won't be tolerated, and specify the sanctions the Army can impose if he or she repeats the blunder. Because your subordinate leaders will do most of the counseling, make sure they know how to counsel soldiers properly. Advise them that while oral counseling is generally appropriate for on-the- spot instances of minor misconduct or substandard performance, it can have two drawbacks: No written record is made, and a verbal reprimand can fade from the soldier's mind.

Written counselings have great value for a commander. Yet, they're seldom used properly—if they're used at all—even though Army regulations require periodic written counselings for all soldiers (officers, noncommissioned officers, and enlisted personnel). Try to be *one* commander who meets this responsibility—do written counselings. Your company will be better for it, and your successor will bless you for the record you've kept. Also, written counseling statements support future actions you might take. Often, they're the evidence that supports adverse administrative, nonjudicial, and judicial actions. These statements should accurately portray a soldier's track record, both good and bad.

Tip

When a platoon leader requests an Article 15 for one of his soldiers, ask to see the soldier's file. If you find no counseling statements, good or bad, have a heart-to-heart chat with your young lieutenant and have him have a chat with the platoon sergeant. If he says, "But sir, this soldier has been told a million times to . . . ," remind the good lieutenant that words "evaporate" the minute they leave the mouth. If you periodically check counseling statements, you'll uncover this problem before it becomes an issue that is "undocumented."

New company commanders usually hesitate to give adverse written counselings or reprimands; instead, they elect to use oral counseling. This practice can lead to greater problems in the long run. The advice is straightforward—the disposition of a soldier's minor misconducts should be gradually elevated: such as oral counseling, written counseling, and letter of admonition or reprimand, and so forth.

War Story

A company commander kept giving oral counselings to a soldier who was frequently in trouble for relatively minor alcohol-related matters. The process continued until one night the soldier got drunk and destroyed all the government furniture in his room. Because of the serious nature of the offense, the commander referred the matter to his battalion commander for a field-grade Article 15. At the Article 15 hearing, the battalion commander reduced the soldier's rank from E4 to E1, and gave him maximum extra duty. Had the company commander used administrative measures other than oral counseling, he might have gotten this particular soldier's attention, corrected his behavior, saved the command and the soldier from an Article 15, and, even better, met the needs of the unit. So don't hesitate to discipline early; it may prevent further misconduct, and save a soldier.

FM 22-101, *Leadership Counseling*, contains sound advice for teaching counseling skills. Make it required reading for your chain of command, and have a training class on the proper use of counseling—even bringing in a professional counselor who could teach your troops some counseling techniques.

EXTRA TRAINING: Extra training is one of the best, but least-used, tools a commander has for dealing with minor misconduct because it teaches proper standards but isn't considered punishment.

One of your soldiers fails to perform preventive maintenance checks and services on his vehicle. If it's a first offense, consider giving the soldier extra training. His extra training might be to perform PMCS on several vehicles after normal duty hours. You don't have to take judicial action for a first act of misconduct, but

Tip be careful how you use extra training to reinforce a learning situation. It's all too easy to use it illegally. This soldier's extra training for neglecting PMCS shouldn't be to clean latrines. (According to AR 27-10, *Military Justice*, "Extra training must relate directly to the deficiency observed and must be oriented to correct that particular deficiency.") The key in this situation is to resolve the matter at the lowest level possible and in the most constructive way to show the soldier what he or she should do in the future.

REHABILITATIVE TRANSFER: Occasionally, a particular soldier may not adapt to a particular company and its leadership. Everything he touches turns to dirt, but he "ain't all bad." If you believe a soldier is salvageable, consider giving him a rehabilitative transfer to let him prove it elsewhere. Move him to another platoon in your company or ask the battalion commander to transfer him to another company in the same battalion. Make sure the transfer and the reasons for the transfer are well-documented and accompany the soldier to the new organization. Again, make sure you follow a legal doctrine, but be sure, too, you give him a fair shake.

BAR TO REENLISTMENT: Many company commanders mistakenly think that bars to reenlistment are last-gasp options. You should judge each individual case on its merits. No minimum number of counselings, offenses, or other matters are required to support a bar to reenlistment. For example, bars to reenlistment are required for overweight soldiers. It's amazing how quickly weight comes off when a soldier realizes he'll be a civilian unless he meets the Army weight standard. Other situations might include indebtedness, chronic substandard performance, and apathy. A company commander can remove a bar to reenlistment anytime he has reason to. If you impose a bar to reenlistment, talk to your lawyer, because you must consider such things as a soldier's grade and time-in-service.

Loss of Discretionary Benefits

The second administrative option available to a commander is taking away discretionary benefits: Denial of pass privileges, quarters allowance, separate rations, and so forth. Select the one option you think will have the most direct benefit to the individual concerned.

DENIAL OF PASS PRIVILEGES: A pass is a privilege, not a right. Some soldiers in the modern volunteer Army forget this distinction. However, you can deny this special benefit to correct misconduct during off-duty time. Although the company commander imposes this measure, a platoon sergeant, platoon leader, or first sergeant usually recommends the action. You should specifically inform the soldier, *in writing*, of a loss of pass privileges. Putting it in writing tends to "memorialize" an action. Make the time period and any physical restrictions very clear in your written notice.

The loss of a privilege can sometimes be a better attention getter than an Article 15 because many soldiers would much rather lose money than their time and freedom. A soldier shouldn't be surprised by a lost privilege. Make sure your soldiers know the unit standards and repercussions if they violate standards.

Adverse Administrative Actions Short of Separation

The third administrative option available to commanders is a group of adverse administrative actions short of elimination, such as relief for cause or removal from a promotion list. These actions, designed to preserve good discipline, can be career stoppers. Normally, you only take these actions after seeking final advice from your battalion commander. Keep him briefed on problems you've handled at your level. When he's not surprised at your decision for administrative action and agrees with that decision, you've earned recognition from him and, probably, your own troops.

Such adverse administrative actions shouldn't come as a surprise to a soldier. Put him on written notice (counseling statement) to expect serious administrative action if he doesn't correct the deficiency. Again, ensure you're on firm legal ground before you do so.

Separation from the Military

The fourth administrative option is separation from the military, the most severe option, because it affects the individual for the rest of his life. Soldiers administratively separated from the Service receive either an honorable, general, or other-than-honorable discharge. The action becomes a permanent part of a soldier's official military record. Denial of a job in the civilian sector may result from an other-than-honorable discharge. In addition, separating a soldier before he completes his obligated service causes the Army to lose its investment.

Once you *decide* to separate, carry through! An unfit soldier hinders your unit's performance, drains your administrative system, and adversely affects unit morale. *Be warned:* Administrative separation proceedings are time–consuming. A soldier is entitled to consult a lawyer before responding to your initiation of administrative separation proceedings. In some cases, he's entitled to have a board decide whether discharge is appropriate. Keep your first sergeant and battalion S-1 and, in some cases, your lawyer working to process the separation. If the processing time becomes lengthy, ask the battalion commander to attach the soldier, for duty only, to a headquarters unit or other activity where he'll come under the close scrutiny of the battalion command sergeant major. Such scrutiny usually will make your task easier, because you've removed the unfit soldier from the unit and provided independent supervision. While you process the administrative separation paperwork (as recommended by AR 601-280, *Reenlistment Program*), ensure a bar to reenlistment precedes the start of a separation action to prevent eliminated soldiers from re-entering the Service or entering the Reserves. Move quickly on high-visibility cases—such as drug abusers, homosexuals, and thieves.

New company commanders often choose administrative elimination proceedings over court-martial proceedings. You often can process certain separations more quickly than courts-martial but, if a soldier deserves to be court-martialed, do it. Don't employ a separation procedure simply because it's the quickest way to remove an unfit soldier. Always take the appropriate action.

War Story

A company commander routinely disposed of drug offenses, including distribution of marijuana (a felony punishable by up to 15 years in prison and a dishonorable discharge) by the Article 15 route and administrative separations. However, the unit always had a high positive urinalysis rate. The soldiers knew that if they used or distributed drugs all they ultimately faced was elimination from the Service under chapter 14, AR 635-200, Personnel Separations—Enlisted Personnel. *As a result, the unit's drug problem escalated when soldiers began to use and sell drugs while on duty. Eventually, two major sellers were caught and prosecuted. At their courts-martial, the evidence showed that more than one-third of the soldiers in the company were active drug abusers. By continually taking lenient actions earlier, the company commander had allowed the problem to get out of hand. Remember, if an administrative separation clearly fails to meet the ends of discipline, take more stringent measures.*

NONJUDICIAL PUNISHMENT OPTIONS:

Use nonjudicial punishment to correct misconduct punishable under the UCMJ. But use it only when administrative options aren't appropriate and court-martial proceedings aren't warranted. Here are your three nonjudicial options:

- Summarized Article 15
- Company-Grade Article 15
- Field-Grade Article 15

Consult with your lawyer on how to impose an Article 15. AR 27- 10 is your best written guide. Here's some practical advice to a company commander imposing a summarized or company-grade Article 15:

DON'T THREATEN: Threatening a soldier with an Article 15 is one of the worst forms of leadership. It encourages soldiers to go through the mechanics of their job, but doesn't inspire unit loyalty. If you impose Article 15 punishment when clearly deserved—without personal rancor and with a clear statement of necessity—you might inspire a soldier to improve by letting him know a one-time offense isn't the end of a career.

DON'T BLUFF: Make sure every Article 15 you give to a soldier would be successfully prosecuted at a court-martial if that soldier refuses the Article 15 and requests a trial. Thoroughly investigate every offense and talk with your legal advisor to ensure you have sufficient evidence to proceed. If your lawyer tells you he can't successfully prosecute the case at court-martial, don't give the Article 15. Take another course of action.

War Story

A new company commander was in the habit of offering Article 15 actions to her soldiers before a thorough investigation. Eventually, two soldiers refused to accept Article 15s and demanded trials. The lawyers' investigation found insufficient evidence to secure a conviction at a court- martial. As a result, the soldiers weren't prosecuted. Soon thereafter, the commander repeated her blunder. Again, the case couldn't be successfully prosecuted at court-martial. Several soldiers then turned down Article 15 actions because they believed the commander wouldn't pursue a court-martial. Eventually, the commander court-martialed several soldiers for minor offenses before the unit understood she meant business. The end result was a drain on unit morale and a loss of respect for military justice.

DON'T GO IT ALONE: Just as you consulted your subordinate chain of command about adverse administrative actions imposed on a soldier, you also should consult them about potential nonjudicial punishment. Let them make a recommendation. Always make the relevant chain of command a part of your Article 15 proceedings.

Remember, you train your junior leaders. They need to learn how to conduct the proceedings; more importantly—they need to be present to answer questions, express their positions, and give their recommendations for punishment if a soldier is found guilty at an Article 15 hearing. Only after the accused, his or her chain of command, and your first sergeant have made statements should you decide what punishment you'll impose if you find a soldier guilty. You'll have to weigh a variety of options and opinions. Always make your decision with this thought in mind: "I did the best I could for the soldier, the unit, and the Army."

DON'T MAKE EXAMPLES: Young company commanders, particularly when assuming command, sometimes impose harsher-than-necessary punishment to get the word out quickly that the new company commander is tough. Making examples is neither fair nor just. Your soldiers will compare offenses and punishments and quickly let everyone know your discipline isn't fair. Let the punishment fit the crime. You should consider a soldier's age, maturity, experience, past record, and potential for future service before making a final decision. If you're fair, firm, and *consistent*, you will earn the unit's respect. Watch out when you're tired or angry; it's easy to overreact. Sleep on it.

Tip

Keep a record of each Article 15 you give. Even though each case must be judged on its own merits, you want to review your actions regularly. Remember, your soldiers are "keeping book" on your punishments.

DON'T FORGET SUSPENSIONS: Suspensions of reduction in grade, forfeiture of pay, restriction, and extra duty can be good disciplinary tools. Suspending the punishment, or part of a punishment, places a soldier on probation. The basic signal you send when you suspend punishment is that you're giving a soldier the chance to prove he can become a productive member of the team again. Suspending punishment now and then has a useful place in the unit judicial process. You can gain a soldier's gratitude and motivate him to become a better soldier. So suspend a punishment, based on the soldier's previous record and attitude. The "war story" that opens with "speaking of suspensions" cites an unusual case, but it shows the value of suspension under certain circumstances.

War Story

Speaking of suspensions, listen to this one. This story is an unusual case, but it shows the value of suspension under certain circumstances.

A Military Police company commander decided to eliminate (via separation) one of his MPs from the service for several recent offenses. Prior to these offenses, the MP was a model soldier. The young commander was stationed in Germany, three hours from his battalion commander. To make matters worse, he also had four outlying platoons. It was the largest MP company in Europe at the time.

Since a field artillery brigade commander had juris-diction over this matter (judicial and administrative actions of this nature were handled on an area jurisdiction basis in Germany), the battalion commander was gener-ally aware of this soldier and the action that would occur, but otherwise was not involved. The brigade commander approved the elimination from the service and the soldier was to depart from Europe on a Sunday.

On the Thursday before his departure, the soldier finally saw the battalion commander, using the com-mander's open-door policy. The soldier stated his case and brought to light inconsistencies in judicial proce-dures. The battalion commander discovered a dramatic mixture of recommended actions on this soldier—the bri-gade and company commander wanted to eliminate the soldier; the brigade command sergeant major and com-pany first sergeant wanted to retain the soldier.

Suffice it to say that the battalion commander flew to the soldier's unit that afternoon. The battalion com-mander requested the brigade commander suspend the elimination for six months. After heated debate, the bri-gade commander, "against his better judgment," ap-proved the six-month suspension.

The battalion commander then rehabilitatively transferred the soldier to another company with this warning: "You're dead meat if you screw up!" Much to the delight of everyone, and the surprise of a few, the soldier became the number one soldier in his platoon and was the company's guidon bearer at the battalion command-er's change-of-command ceremony a year later.

DON'T FORGET MITIGATION AND REMISSION: Mitigation and remission are reductions in either the qual-ity or quantity of punishment. Either mitigation or remis-sion is appropriate when soldiers, by their subsequent good conduct, merit leniency. For example, you can mitigate a re-duction from E4 to E3 to a forfeiture of pay. Or you can remit (cancel) a suspended forfeiture of pay. Using mitigation and remission sends a powerful signal to other soldiers: One mistake won't ruin a soldier's career in *your* unit if he or she "soldiers back" from misconduct. Consult your lawyer before mitigating or remitting a punishment because you must follow certain rules.

War Story

A young specialist received a company-grade Article 15 for drunk and disorderly conduct. Before this offense, he was a unit superstar ready to go before the sergeant promotion board at battalion headquarters the next month. However, when he was drunk enough one day to insult and curse the unit staff duty NCO before passing out, the company commander took action.

The young specialist's punishment included 14 days of extra duty and 14 days of restriction. Since he'd been an outstanding soldier before this incident, he was deeply embarrassed. After the incident, he worked harder at his job. When punishment was imposed, he continued to work hard and took his extra duty requirements very seriously. He so impressed his chain of command that the unit commander remitted his last three days of extra duty and restriction.

For field-grade Article 15 actions, you'll have to ask the battalion commander to mitigate or remit punishments imposed. If you can justify your reason, normally the battalion commander will have no problem mitigating and remitting certain punishments. Mitigation and remission are excellent ways to tell a soldier you appreciate his hard work and professionalism under adverse conditions.

In the nonjudicial punishment arena, you're the judge and jury. The responsibility of your task demands total professionalism. Continue to seek legal advice from your Judge Advocate and support from your chain of command.

COURT-MARTIAL OPTIONS:

Use a court-martial for the most serious violations of the Uniform Code of Military Justice. A commander recommends to court-martial a soldier when adverse administrative actions and nonjudicial punishment are inadequate and don't meet the ends of justice. You may recommend four court-martial options:

- Summary
- Special
- Special (Bad Conduct Discharge)
- General

Court-martial, more than administrative or nonjudicial actions, demands legal assistance. Basically, if you elect to court-martial at the bad conduct discharge, special, or general court-martial level, you've decided the offending soldier, if convicted, deserves to risk going to prison or receiving a punitive discharge. Moreover, a conviction by a special or general court-martial is a federal conviction and stays with a soldier for life. Court-martial proceedings are a drain on your time and your unit's time. Court-martial is a serious matter. You should undertake it only after **legal** and **command** advice.

Military Justice Decisionmaking Considerations

BE TIMELY: Investigate, consult your lawyer, confer with the chain of command, and initiate action. The longer you wait, the less effective your punishment will be for the soldier and the unit. Dragging the matter out indicates indecisiveness, and an indecisive commander needs a staff position, not a command.

BE FAIR AND EQUITABLE: Do what's right for the *individual*, your company, and the Army. Sometimes, dropping the hammer on a good soldier whose first mistake is a serious one is hard. Hard decisions test your resolve, however, and let your soldiers know what kind of leader you are. If a bad apple remains a problem while he's awaiting administrative action, transfer him. You're being unfair to the rest of the unit if you don't take decisive action.

BE FIRM AND CONSISTENT: A unit with firm disciplinary standards is a good unit. If a soldier knows he'll pay for misconduct, he'll think twice before he acts. Likewise, if he knows he'll be rewarded for good actions, he'll think twice about misconduct. Make sure your soldiers know from day one that you're a firm, consistent disciplinarian. Take consistent actions—no matter who commits an act of misconduct: enlisted, NCO, or officer.

★ ★ ★ ★ ★ *THE BRASS SAYS*

Lieutenant General Andrew Chambers on discipline: A company commander must gain and maintain *control* of his company. Discipline is the key. A soldier must know what the standards are and at all times be required to meet them. But he also must know that he has a firm, just, and caring commander. Let your actions do your talking.

JUDGE EACH CASE ON ITS OWN MERITS: If you're fair, and consistent, you will always judge each case on its own merits. Your sense of fair play and your consistency in exercising that sense are the keys.

BE AWARE OF THE MESSAGES YOU SEND: Every soldier won't know about all circumstances of a particular judicial incident; therefore, perceptions of favoritism can result. Undercut those perceptions by ensuring your unit receives military justice classes that explain how the system works. Tell your soldiers, too, they must value the soldier's privacy and your judgment. They should not make hasty judgments based just on their quick estimates of a case.

Tip An infantry company commander had two soldiers miss guard duty on the same night. It was Jones's first act of misconduct during his two years in the unit. However, it was Smith's third guard duty absence in six months. The hard-charging commander gave Jones a summarized Article 15.

He gave Smith a company-grade Article 15 and reduced him one rank. Because the unit soldiers weren't aware of the different circumstances of Jones and Smith, a perception of partiality resulted. It didn't help matters that Jones was the unit "brownnoser." How do you counter a negative perception? Use the members of your chain of command. They'll be present at your Article 15 hearings. To help set the record straight, have your chain of command brief the troops on why Smith and Jones received different punishments. Whatever you do, however, don't dismiss negative perceptions lightly. They can simmer for a long time, often leading to a loss of confidence in the chain of command and a decrease in morale.

BE AWARE OF REPERCUSSIONS OF YOUR DECISIONS: "Business as usual" doesn't happen when you take adverse action against a soldier. Adverse actions affect individuals, their families, and the whole unit. Be especially sensitive if your unit has exceptional esprit de corps; many of your soldiers may resent an adverse action simply because it reflects poorly on the unit.

Making Your Decision

CONDUCT AS THOROUGH AN INVESTIGATION AS THE OFFENSE WARRANTS: Deal with trifles quickly; deal with more serious matters thoroughly. "GET IT IN WRITING," with sworn statements for more serious incidents. Get reports that answer the who, what, where, when, and how of the incident. Return the report to the investigator if it's incomplete, and establish a suspense for the reply.

CONSULT: Once you have the facts, get advice from your legal counselor. Before you act, touch base with those in your subordinate chain of command who should be included in the investigation. Are you and the first sergeant on the same wave length? Do you need to consult the battalion commander for his advice?

LET THE ACCUSED TALK: Good commanders keep open minds. Sometimes, the "accused" presents a totally different case from the one presented to you in the investigation. After properly advising the accused of his legal rights, give the accused every opportunity to explain his side. Once you give a soldier the chance for a full and detailed explanation, you may need to investigate further. Make time to investigate his or her version; it's one more step to ensure complete justice.

MAKE THE DECISION: Once you have all the information, make your decision without fear. If you've done your homework, you'll have no problem if a soldier appeals his punishment. However, know why you made your decision, because you may have to justify that decision on appeal. If you agonize over your military justice decision, FINE. It means YOU CARE! But if you agonize to the point of indecision, not so fine. You stumble, and your unit suffers. Therefore, make an informed, but prompt decision.

Let's go back to the beginning for a moment . . .

Remember your sergeant first class's misconduct?
- What will you do, Company Commander?
- What type of disciplinary action will you recommend for your silent platoon sergeant?
- Should he lose a stripe? (Can your battalion commander reduce a sergeant first class?)
- Should he be relieved and rehabilitatively transferred to another company?
- How are you going to help him with his drinking problem?
- What organizations are available to help you help him?
- What effect will this decision have on his family?
- How do the female soldiers feel who have been accosted by this man?
- What effect will this incident have on the rest of your company, especially the lower enlisted soldiers?

Answer these questions in light of what you've read in this chapter. If you don't know the answers to these questions, you should know where to find them.

The Bottom Line
for
Military Justice and Administrative Law

- JUDICIAL DECISIONS AREN'T MADE IN A VACUUM—Lawyers, battalion commanders, first sergeants, and subordinates all contribute to making smart decisions.

- JUDICIAL OBJECTIVES—Once you've decided to punish, rehabilitate, or eliminate, choose the appropriate option to obtain results best for the soldier and the unit.

- COUNSELING—An adverse oral counseling often evaporates the minute it leaves your mouth. Written counseling, however, is the basis for almost any legal or administrative action.

- SEPARATE UNFIT SOLDIERS—Don't waste your time and the Army's money on unfit soldiers. An unfit soldier is like a fungus—the longer he stays, the more your unit rots.

- DON'T threaten, bluff, or make examples when offering an Article 15.

- COMPASSION does have a place in the Army! Use it wisely.

- JUDICIAL ACTIONS administered firmly, fairly, timely, and consistently are your obligation—and your soldier's right.

- JUDGE each case on its own merits!

- ALWAYS, ALWAYS, ALWAYS allow every soldier his day in court.

- REMEMBER, you have to go to sleep at night knowing you did what was RIGHT—RIGHT for the soldier and RIGHT for the Army.

Bibliography for
Military Justice and Administrative Law

AR 27-10, *Military Justice*.

AR 601-280, *Reenlistment Program*.

AR 635-200, *Personnel Separations—Enlisted Personnel*.

FM 22-101, *Leadership Counseling*.

FM 27-1, *Legal Guide for Commanders*.

5. Personnel and Administration

People are your most precious asset; neglect them, and you're doomed to fail.

The Author

THIS COULD HAPPEN TO YOU—Getting Noncommissioned Officer Evaluation Reports (NCO-ERs) in on time is a high-priority item in your battalion. You've been in command four months and are starting to feel comfortable with your ability to do the job. The real test is coming—the battalion inspection of your company next week. Everyone in your unit has been working overtime to get ready. Then, the battalion chaplain comes to talk with you.

Apparently, your new personnel sergeant went to the chaplain with a serious problem. She discovered four NCO-ERs were misplaced three months ago. The orderly room hadn't sent them to the raters; consequently, the NCO-ERs were hopelessly late. She's aware of the battalion inspection next week and your emphasis on prompt submission of efficiency reports. She even remembers when you told her about your introductory conversation with the battalion commander. Specifically, he told you that you were taking command of a pretty good unit, but the orderly room was a disaster and personnel actions were routinely lost or late. He wanted you to take a *personal* interest and fix the problem. He put most of the blame on your weak first sergeant, because he felt the 1SG didn't properly supervise the orderly room. The battalion commander told the first sergeant to improve or he'd be history.

Your personnel sergeant went to the chaplain because when she informed the first sergeant of the late NCO-ERs, he went ballistic. He put the blame on her when, in fact, she'd only been in the job a month. He told her to do whatever it took to hide the mistake from the battalion inspection team next week, or he'd probably be relieved if the error were found. She was frightened and didn't know where to go other than the chaplain's office. The chaplain received her permission to talk to you about this matter.

NOW WHAT HAPPENS, COMPANY COMMANDER?

- Do you tell your battalion commander now or hope the inspection team doesn't find the late NCO-ERs?
- If the team does, is your first sergeant's career ruined? How about your status?
- What about your personnel sergeant? What do you say to her?

These are some of the questions that should be racing through your mind. Before answering, however, you should fully understand your responsibility in personnel and administration. With understanding and a *firm* conviction to always **do what is right**, you'll handle the problem and increase the unit's morale.

The Company Commander's Personnel and Administration Responsibilities

Always put the **PERSON** in personnel. You have two major responsibilities: Efficient processing of your soldiers' *personnel actions*, and establishing effective *personnel management* programs. The service you provide soldiers in these areas follows them through their careers.

The key to your success in personnel and administration is to know when to get personally involved. If in doubt, get involved. Your personal involvement sends a powerful message to your soldiers: You **CARE**.

PERSONNEL ACTIONS: Your *insistence* that all personnel actions be completed promptly and accurately is your obligation to your soldiers. Award recommendations, leave approvals, reenlistments, and compassionate reassignments are personnel actions you must handle properly. Each action has a direct effect on a soldier's morale and, eventually, the morale of your entire unit.

PERSONNEL MANAGEMENT: Personnel management is the proper handling of group or organizational personnel programs, rather than individual actions. Promotion policy, the sponsorship program, and the equal opportunity program fall in this category. Your job is to ensure these programs operate fairly and are clearly understood by all soldiers.

(NOTE: This chapter assumes you command a separate company with your own orderly room and no Personnel and Administrative Center (PAC). As you are aware, if you have the services of a PAC, your orderly room responsibilities "should be" significantly decreased.)

Educate Yourself

REVIEW REGULATIONS AND INSPECTION REPORTS: Have a good working knowledge of personnel regulations. Each day, you'll handle such actions as promotions, separation actions, and reenlistments. The greater your understanding of the rules, the less time you spend researching regulations. The personnel and administration area has more regulations than any other function in your company.

For example, TC 12-17, *Adjutant's Call, the S-1 Handbook*, has 15 pages of references listed by subject and cross-referenced by numeric designation. Get a copy of this list of references and keep it handy, because it provides an overview for manuals you may need. You should keep five key personnel manuals in your office:

- *All Ranks Personnel Update.*
- *Officer Ranks Personnel Update.*
- *Enlisted Ranks Personnel Update.*
- *Personnel Evaluations Update.*
- DA Pam 600-8, *Management and Administration Procedures.*

These manuals are your *primary* personnel references. Be familiar with their tables of contents. As problems develop, requiring you to review certain regulations, dig deep, research well, and become an authority. In addition, these regulations will enable you to check your orderly room's work.

In about six months, you'll gain most of the working knowledge you need to do your job. From that point on, a case-by-case review will suffice.

If your first sergeant and personnel sergeant know less about these regulations than you do, you're in deep trouble. Correct the problem immediately.

Review your last two battalion personnel and administration inspection reports, the last Inspector General (IG) report, and the last Material Assistance and Inspection Team (MAIT) report. These two documents should give you a clear view of your personnel administration status. Normally, the MAIT report discusses your publications. Zero in on recurring deficiencies. As you become familiar with your orderly room, check to ensure these deficiencies are corrected. If they aren't, ask your first sergeant and administrative NCO why. *Top-notch units rarely have recurring deficiencies.*

Tip Look closely at the recommendation-for-improvement section of inspection reports. Many times, a valid recommendation gets overlooked. Remember, experts usually do the inspecting and, over the years, have seen the best and worst way to go about every task imaginable. If your personnel section has ignored key recommendations and several recurring deficiencies remain, you need to get more involved. Once you get everyone's attention, you can back off.

TALK WITH KEY INDIVIDUALS: Talk first with your battalion adjutant/S-1 and battalion personnel sergeant. They not only write the battalion inspection report, they also are your first contacts at battalion headquarters. They can easily highlight strengths, weaknesses, and capabilities of your orderly room personnel. Ask their advice on what they'd do (if anything) to change your orderly room. If you form a professional relationship, these two individuals can keep you out of hot water. Because you have more than your fair share of opportunities to fail at personnel actions, you need all the help available. Remember, *efficient service to the soldier is paramount.*

Also talk with your battalion command sergeant major. He's often the hidden link in the personnel business. He has the ear of the battalion commander and can help you fill your key personnel shortages. Insist that your first sergeant constantly reconcile your unit's personnel problems with the battalion/squadron CSM.

War Story

*A cavalry squadron commander in Europe put his command sergeant major in charge of all enlisted assignments. (Although the exception rather than the rule, in this case it worked.) This arrangement left little room for a "we-they" mentality to develop between the companies and the battalion. As a result, the company commanders and the squadron CSM communicated. The squadron commander allowed no disagreements to reach his desk. The problems were either resolved between the company commanders and squadron CSM or nothing happened. The squadron commander acted only on coordinated recommendations. The squadron commander's teaching point was "**Don't put your boss in a position to choose between two right hands.**"*

Talk to your fellow company commanders. More than likely, they've experienced several situations that, if the opportunity arose again, they'd handle differently. Capture those experiences and ask questions:

- What were your biggest personnel problems when you assumed command?
- What advice can you give me to ensure that my orderly room serves the soldier?
- What personnel role should I expect from my first sergeant?
- What other agencies, besides the battalion headquarters, have you found helpful in solving your personnel problems?
- What are the battalion commander's pet peeves in personnel and administration?
- Do you have any "tricks of the trade" or successful programs to help you with personnel and administration?

Once you have answers to these questions, you're now ready to talk with your battalion commander. Have your "ducks in a row" and prepare specific personnel and administrative questions to ask him. Your goal is to find out his expectations of your unit in this specific area. Don't leave his office until you're satisfied you have answers to all your questions.

VISIT KEY ORGANIZATIONS: Visit your personnel service company or center (PSC). Talk with the commander and find out your unit's track record and what suggestions she may have for improvement. Discuss the major pitfalls most units experience and how they correct them. Ask if the PSC provides assistance teams. Have her give you an organizational briefing so you know exactly what her organization does and how your unit should interface. Visit the PSC commander every month or two to ensure you stay ahead of potential problems.

Visit your local finance commander. Ask similar questions of him. He, as well as the PSC commander, will be more than glad to assist you—after all, the better prepared you are to do your job, the easier the task for their units. Check your sure-pay statistics with the finance officer and also ask if his staff would brief your subordinate chain of command on leave and earning statements— what everyone calls the LES.(We'll discuss the LES later in this chapter.) Take advantage of his experience and cultivate a relationship to last throughout your command tour.

Four "Hot" Personnel Areas

1—STANDARD INSTALLATION/DIVISION PERSON-NEL SYSTEM (SIDPERS): Your first instinct might be to tell your first sergeant, "Handle it . . . I can't be bothered." Wrong response! SIDPERS is the cornerstone of personnel and financial reports in your unit. You don't have to be an expert, but you need to know enough to keep your SIDPERS clerk "honest."

What is SIDPERS? It's an automated, personnel data system that gives you information about your soldiers and your unit so you can do a better job. SIDPERS links the personnel system from your unit to the Department of the Army. According to DA Pam 600-8-1, *SIDPERS Unit Level Procedures*, SIDPERS has three major functions:

- Strength Accounting (gains and losses).
- Personnel Management (organizational and personnel record keeping).
- System Interface (informational exchange with other automated systems at higher headquarters).

2—SIDPERS REPORTS: There are approximately 69 different command and staff SIDPERS reports. Luckily for you, not all apply at the company level. Your orderly room has a SIDPERS clerk whose primary job is to handle your unit's strength accounting records. Your first sergeant also should be proficient in this field. But all this high-powered talent doesn't absolve you of overall responsibility. Use DA Pam 600-8, *Management and Administrative Procedures*, to check the following key SIDPERS reports that come across your desk:

- **Unit Manning Report** (UMR). The UMR places the "face with the space." Use it to monitor use and assignment of personnel. If your soldiers aren't properly slotted on the UMR, you may lose them as overages.

War Story

A unit commander required her first sergeant and platoon sergeants to reconcile the Unit Manning Report each month before she'd sign it. In turn, she and the platoon leaders would reconcile the UMR quarterly. She drew her entire chain of command into the personnel picture.

- **Personnel Qualification Roster** (PQR). The PQR is a detailed listing of personnel information on the soldiers in your unit.
- **Personnel Strength Zero Balance.** This report compares the SIDPERS personnel file strength data with the strength data your unit submits. Use the zero balance report to resolve your strength discrepancies. Reconcile it monthly and ensure it's balanced.
- **Enlisted Promotion Report** (CO1). Commonly referred to as the CO1, the Enlisted Promotion Report lists soldiers eligible for promotion with or without waivers. Check the data on this report closely; otherwise, your soldiers may not be promoted when deserved.

Tip

Inspectors normally look at the Enlisted Promotion Report very closely. Uncorrected errors indicate your personnel folks are not taking care of your soldiers. You can't talk your way out of this one.

Keys to successful SIDPERS management:

- Ensure all SIDPERS reports are ACCURATE and TIMELY.
- Employ the ONE-DAY RULE—forward all SIDPERS transactions, supporting documents, and so forth to the SIDPERS interface branch no later than the first duty day after the effective date of the change.
- Check your SIDPERS clerk's and 1SG's work— especially on the reports listed above.
- Don't be one-person deep in SIDPERS: Cross-train to have a back-up SIDPERS clerk.

Tip A wise commander cross-trains his *entire* orderly room so that everyone knows how to process awards, NCO-ERs, SIDPERS, and other personnel actions. He also lets everyone know that he expects time-sensitive personnel requirements to be met. "Help each other out when there's a close deadline" are the magic words. In particular, protect your personnel clerk when suspenses approach.

The welfare of your soldiers is too important for you and your first sergeant to neglect SIDPERS. DA Pam 600-8-20, *SIDPERS Handbook for Commanders*, is the basic, easily understood guide on SIDPERS. Review it. Now and then ask your SIDPERS clerk how things are going. Let him or her speak freely. You'll learn not only how things are going, but how well that clerk is performing.

3—NONCOMMISSIONED OFFICER EVALUATION REPORTS (NCO-ERs): Hear Ye, Hear Ye, Hear Ye! The NCO-ER is *the* most important document in an enlisted soldier's record. It's the single most important document in determining promotions, school selections, and assignments. Treat your NCO-ER responsibility as second to none. AR 623-205, *Enlisted Evaluation Reporting System*, is your guidebook. Here's how *you* should operate:

- Write the NCO-ER as if it were your own.
- Submit NCO-ERs on time. A late NCO-ER indicates a system failure and you're responsible for the system.

Tip On the rare occasions when you have a late NCO-ER, always alert your battalion commander. Never, *never* simply forward a late NCO-ER without notifying him. Be prepared to "take a hit" yourself, if you deserve it.

- Your system is vital. You need an effective, manageable, NCO-ER processing and tracking system. Your entire chain of command must know the system and adhere to its guidelines. Hold people's feet to the fire! Don't rely on higher headquarters to remind you when an NCO-ER is due. Make your unit leadership track *their* soldiers. In fact, keep a master tracking system in your orderly room.

● Publish your rating chain. Keep it updated.

● Never surprise a soldier by an adverse NCO-ER. If your system works right, he'll know it's coming because he's already been counseled, in writing.

● Write an NCO-ER with concern. Writing an NCO-ER the day before it's due is bad practice. Write a rough draft at least 10 days before the report is due. Let it sit. Then pick it up and *rewrite* it. This practice ultimately will *save* you time and will produce more accurate NCO-ERs for your soldiers. Give yourself time to do it right. *And* give your boss time to do his portion.

War Story

A company commander gave his battalion commander less than a day to write the senior rater portion of his first sergeant's NCO-ER. The battalion commander stopped what he was doing and completed the NCO-ER to ensure that it was on time. He took considerable time writing his portion, because the evaluation concerned an exceptional 1SG, who deserved promotion to SGM. The battalion commander also had to get the brigade commander, as the reviewer, to sign the NCO-ER. So the battalion commander and his boss were both caught in a time jam by the company commander's laxity. They both did their jobs as responsible senior commanders to take care of an outstanding first sergeant. Then the battalion commander provided a "significant emotional event" in the company commander's life, to ensure that this problem never occurred again. Smart people only get burned once.

When writing NCO-ERs, also consider these points:

● Use specific facts. Too many times, NCO-ERs read like greeting cards. If you don't have specific facts, ask the soldier for them.

● Pull the trigger. Demand that all NCO-ERs be presented to the ratee in person. The worst mistake is to forward an individual's NCO-ER through distribution. If you or your chain of command can't present an NCO-ER in person, especially an adverse NCO-ER, you have no business being leaders.

● Review all NCO-ERs written in your company. You'll ensure your soldiers are properly cared for and find out if any people in your unit need help in writing NCO-ERs. Include your 1SG in the review process. (He should be the second most knowledgeable person in your unit on how to write NCO-ERs.) The battalion adjutant and CSM can advise you as well. Be sure they review an NCO-ER *before* the rated soldier sees it. Give yourself time to review their suggestions and make your changes *before* you present it to the soldier.

● Follow the NCO counseling procedures (DA Form 2166-7-1) to the letter of the law. It's the best improvement to the NCO evaluation system in years.

● Remember Special NCO-ERs. A Special NCO-ER is an excellent way to recognize particularly outstanding deeds. Take care of your best soldiers; they're the soldiers you want to be the future Command Sergeant Majors of the Army.

4—OFFICER EVALUATION REPORTS (OERs): The Officer Evaluation Report is the most important document in an officer's record. It affects officer promotions, school selections, and assignments. Guidelines for the NCO-ER apply equally to the OER. Look at AR 623-105, *Officer Evaluation Reporting System*, for the mechanics of the form. You also need to understand the importance of the support form and the senior rater section:

OER SUPPORT FORM: Complete the OER support form within the first 30 days of the rating period. Follow these general guidelines:

● Have a *face-to-face* discussion with the rated officer about his duties and performance objectives. Tell him what you expect—*clearly*. Then let him talk and you'll learn what's on his mind.

• If you're the *rated* officer, ask to see a copy of your rater's support form in order to guide you in determining your duties and objectives. As company commander, ask the battalion adjutant or executive officer to give you a copy of the battalion commander's support form. Remember—do so within the first 30 days.

• Keep the support form up to date, as duties and objectives change. This duty is another form of footlocker counseling.

Tip Every three to four months, make a point to review and update the support forms of the lieutenants you rate. A review doesn't take that long and it will keep both parties focused on "agreed-upon" duties and objectives. Consider using the support form during counseling sessions. Don't let the support form simply sit until the evaluation period ends and an OER is required.

• Complete block 4C, the "contributions" section of the support form, with considerable thought. The goal is to list contributions in such a fashion that the rater can use most of the statements from the support form on the OER itself.

SENIOR RATER SECTION: The senior rater section has reduced inflation in the OER system and become the "big discriminator" in the OER. The section consists of the senior rater profile and the senior rater narrative. A company commander normally isn't a senior rater, but it won't hurt you to understand what the senior rater must do:

• Normally, a rater recommends the block a senior rater should use on an OER.

• The block checked is meaningless without the senior rater profile. A good senior rater uses the "center of mass" or "pack" concept to determine his senior rater profile. The "pack" refers to the most frequently checked box. The senior rater makes an assessment—Is the rated officer:

- Ahead of the "pack"?
- With the "pack"?
- Behind the "pack"?

• Senior rater narratives are important. Don't be offended if the senior rater narrative section isn't filled. The more concise, the better. It's not how much you say; it's how well you say it. Often, all that needs to be said can be said in four or five lines.

A good rater will ensure he takes care of a good commander. In other words, your fate is in your battalion commander's hands; the fate of your lieutenants is in your hands. Inform your battalion commander of the progress of each of your lieutenants. When you recommend a particular senior rater block for LT "X," it shouldn't come as a surprise to the battalion commander or to LT "X."

Personnel Actions

The personnel area can be frustrating, bureaucratic, and time-consuming, but its benefits to the soldier are obvious. Seven personnel actions you need to watch closely are: *Awards, Reenlistments, Hometown News Releases, Leaves, Meal Cards, Flagging Actions, and Unit Transmittal Letters*.

★ ★ ★ ★ ★ *THE BRASS SAYS*

Major General Eugene Cromartie on the personnel system: *Challenge* the personnel system to the Nth degree—especially if it is in the best interest of your troops. Don't take no for an answer. Your troops deserve your perseverance.

AWARDS: Preparing an award recommendation takes time, but it's a "money maker." Soldiers want to and should be recognized for their hard work. Besides, most people respond better to positive strokes than to negative ones.

★ ★ ★ ★ ★ *THE BRASS SAYS*

Napoleon on awards: A soldier will fight long and hard for a bit of colored ribbon.

You have three award responsibilities:

• Ensure every soldier is *considered* for an award.

• Ensure all awards are prepared properly, submitted on time, and presented before departure. Not only is the soldier recognized in front of his peers and supervisors, but other soldiers in your unit also see that a good job earns a reward.

• Ensure the soldier's military personnel records jacket (MPRJ) properly reflects the award.

Stay on top of your awards procedures. Make sure you have a suspense system (modeled on your OER and EER suspense system) that ensures you consider everyone for an award. If the chain of command considers a particular soldier for an award, but recommends disapproval (with your support), inform that soldier in *writing* why he didn't receive an award. If your counseling system is already effective, this negative decision won't come as a surprise.

Awards exist for service, achievement, and retirement. Another kind of achievement award exists, too. It's usually overlooked, yet can be very effective. It's commonly called the "impact" award. An impact award is an achievement award approved and presented *on the spot*, before submitting the request for an award (DA Form 638). However, you must get verbal permission from the approving authority before you present it. For example, a company commander requests his battalion commander's permission to present an Army Achievement Medal for a particularly significant accomplishment. The company commander then sends the completed DA Form 638 to his commander after the fact. Impact awards provide immediate recognition for outstanding work. The company commanders who use impact awards as incentives usually are the best. Be one of them. You don't want to hand out impact awards every day but, when the achievement calls for one, make sure you do it.

War Story

A battalion commander finished his quarterly inspection of one of his units and, as usual, the second platoon was the best. For the third time in a row, Sergeant First Class (SFC) Flowers, the platoon sergeant, guided his soldiers to this top rating, despite the absence of a platoon leader. To recognize this achievement, the company commander re- quested *the battalion commander give an Army Achievement Medal impact award to SFC Flowers. He further suggested the presentation occur* right away . . . *at the exit brief. The battalion commander thought it was a great idea and personally pinned on the medal in front of the entire unit leadership. It was a total surprise to everyone present. SFC Flowers was speechless. Everyone else took note: Work hard and you do get rewarded in* this *company.*

Recognition can be a powerful motivator. But it takes imagination:

War Story

A new company commander was in charge of an MP unit at a Corps headquarters in Europe. He knew such units are always *visible. (The* Battalion *commander, the* Bri- gade *commander, and the* Corps Commander—and their staffs—notice the MPs every day, especially on gate duty.) At this headquarters, the Corps Commander regularly ate his MP subordinate commanders alive because of medi- ocre performance of the command's MPs. The sound of bodies being devoured quickly funneled its way down the chain of command. The sharp young company com- mander decided to fix the problem quickly, rather than face the dragon's jaws. He developed an incentive awards program for the MPs, based on incident-free duty hours.*

Incident-free duty hours	Award
200	Letter of Appreciation from company commander
300	Battalion Certificate of Appreciation
420	Battalion Certificate of Achievement (5 promotion points)
850	Brigade Certificate of Achievement (5 promotion points)
1,300	Army Achievement Medal (AAM)(15 promotion points) and a 3-day pass
2,400	Army Commendation Medal (ARCOM) (20 promotion points) and a 4-day pass

An MP performing this duty would receive the ARCOM in about eight months. The program worked, because it gave the MPs something positive to work toward. Every time they went on duty, they had a chance to build up credit, not merely avoid a butt-chewing. Consequently, their diligence, morale, and appearance improved quickly. And the Corps Commander's fearful snarl softened into an occasional growl.

Don't let the mechanics for award submissions stifle you. Use the system for completing the DA Form 638. Ensure the NCO in charge of your orderly room understands that system. Your battalion adjutant should be an expert on the proper way to submit award requests. Consult him and obtain sample write-ups for each kind of award.

Don't forget the awards *ceremony*, the icing on the cake. Make it first class:

- Give advance notice to the recipient and the unit. Schedule the ceremony when most of the unit can attend.

- Invite the recipient's family, friends, and associates to the ceremony.
- Invite the battalion commander and command sergeant major when appropriate.
- Have a photographer present and make sure the recipient gets copies of the pictures. Post several copies of pictures on the unit bulletin board.
- Prepare your remarks *in advance*. Don't "wing it." Know the recipient's specific accomplishments.
- Have a pre-printed hometown news release completed and ready for the soldier's signature.

Awards ceremonies are special occasions. Take the time to do them right.

Tip After the ceremony, take a minute or two to *write* a note to the recipient's parents (or spouse if he or she wasn't able to attend the ceremony), informing them of the award and what a great soldier their son or daughter (or spouse) is. Take that extra step toward caring leadership. For example:

Dear Mr. and Mrs. Jones,

Your daughter, Susan, is a terrific soldier. I just presented her the Army Achievement Medal for winning the enlisted Soldier of the Quarter competition for the second consecutive quarter. Her accomplishment is significant because . . .

State specific instances . . . don't write a fill-in-the-blank letter!

War Story

One successful company commander had the habit of acknowledging the entire squad or platoon in which an individual earned an award. For example, if a soldier in the 3rd squad, 4th platoon won the Soldier of the Quarter competition, the commander also gave the 3rd squad a day off. The technique quickly increased unit integrity and cohesion. It became one "tight" unit.

Don't ever underestimate the power and influence of an "atta-boy" or "atta-girl." And handle it right, each and every time.

REENLISTMENT: Reenlistment is a privilege earned by good performance. Your goal is to reenlist only quality soldiers. Set the stage early. "Dirt bags" need not apply! Reenlistment isn't solely your responsibility. It should involve your entire chain of command. Thus, you should inspect the reenlistment data card file monthly. Determine who is or isn't doing the required interviews. A "friendly" chat should fix any problems. If your chain of command sees you're serious about reenlistment and that you conduct *your* interviews, they'll follow suit.

Speaking of interviews, consider these points:

- Do some research before the interview. Know the soldier and his or her options.
- Interview each soldier separately. Group reenlistment interviews don't work.
- Keep the interview informal. In fact, not every interview has to be in your office. Pull one of your mechanics aside in the motor pool for a chat about his future opportunity.
- Set yourself a quota of interviews for each week. Tell your retention NCO to "bug" you, if necessary, to do your interviews.
- Spend extra time with the winners. Don't waste your time on losers.
- Make it hard for a winner to say no. But if he has sound reasons for getting out, fully support him. Then, shift gears and talk to him about benefits of the Reserve Components.

Establish a reenlistment incentive program and ceremony. You should treat the ceremony the same as an awards ceremony—**first class.** Numerous incentive items are available for the reenlistee, such as unit T-shirts, unit mugs, and three-day passes. Package the incentives and the ceremony together and you can have a superb reenlistment incentive program.

Your reenlistment NCO probably is doing this work as an additional duty. The reenlistment NCO deserves this support:

- Proper training.
- Sufficient time and resources.
- Total chain of command support.
- Assistance from the "full-time" battalion retention NCO.
- Easy access to you and your 1SG to resolve problems.
- Recognition for good work.

HOMETOWN NEWS RELEASE (HTNR): Unfortunately, commanders rarely see the hometown news release pay off; consequently, many don't support the program. The HTNR program tells the public of your soldier's accomplishment, and, at the same time, advertises the Army. Remember, it's *mandatory* to have an HTNR *program*, but your soldiers' participation is voluntary. Consequently, make completing the HTNR form (DD Form 2266) as easy as possible. Give your soldier a short cover letter explaining the program, a sample of a completed DD Form 2266, and a blank form for him to complete. A sample cover letter is included in TC 12-17, *Adjutant's Call, The S-1 Handbook*. Fill in as much of the DD Form 2266 as you can to help the soldier and promote the program. Your battalion adjutant should be able to help you develop an organized, painless system.

Activities and accomplishments worth an HTNR:

- Assignment to or departure from the unit.
- Promotion or selection as Soldier of the Quarter.
- Receipt of an award.
- School selection.
- Perfect PT score.
- Safe driving record.
- Participation in special exercises.
- Individual or team member in a championship sporting event.

If possible, include the soldier's spouse in the release. A spouse contributes to a soldier's success. Families, friends, and relatives like to see their loved ones in print.

They won't see their soldier in print, however, unless **you** get involved.

LEAVE: Everyone needs a break from the everyday hassles of work. However, in our "can do" Army, many often ignore the military's generous leave policy. Sometimes we work—and allow our subordinates to work—too hard.

Encourage your soldiers to use their 30 days of authorized leave each year. Set the example: use yours. If you don't take leave, your subordinates may misinterpret it as a signal of your lack of confidence in their ability to do the job in your absence—the last perception you want to create. Remember, no one is indispensable—not even you.

Ask your 1SG to have the unit's leave and earning statements checked each month and tell you who needs to take leave. And earmark those soldiers who are in the hole on leave; don't let them get in over their heads.

Be familiar with sign-out procedures, so you can check to ensure your orderly room personnel correctly charge your soldiers for the leave they take, and your soldiers aren't charged for leave they didn't take—leave equates to money.

MEAL CARDS: The key to success with meal cards is strict accountability. Meal cards have CASH value and you must account for their issue, use, withdrawal, replacement, and destruction— everything! Make sure your clerk follows AR 600-38, *Meal Card Management*, to the letter and periodically checks the accounting procedure.

Any soldier with a meal card is entitled to reimbursement if he misses a meal because of duty. Have him complete DD Form 1475, *Missed Meals*, and the Finance Office will adjust his paycheck accordingly. As a general rule, your clerk won't want to be bothered with missed meals; they're another "paperwork" hassle. Insist on an aggressive reimbursement program, because money "talks" and you care.

FLAGGING ACTIONS: A flagging action normally is a negative action. Among its many uses, you may have reason to flag a soldier who is pending reassignment, possibly delaying his departure. More typically, you may have to flag a soldier who enters the Army weight control program. The "flag" makes him ineligible for favorable personnel actions, such as promotion, reenlistment, and schooling, until it is lifted, such as when the soldier is disenrolled from the weight-control program.

All kinds of horror stories exist about soldiers whose flags weren't lifted at the appropriate time. Commanders have a tendency to flag quickly (it does get someone's attention) and then *forget to remove the flag*. In this case, a soldier has a valid complaint for the chain of command or the inspector general.

Be as quick to remove the flag as you are to flag a soldier. And check with your lawyer **before** flagging a soldier, particularly when dealing with investigations and courts-martial.

UNIT TRANSMITTAL LETTER (UTL): The Unit Transmittal Letter is the document your orderly room sends to the Personnel Service Company (PSC) or Finance and Accounting Office (FAO) on personnel actions affecting your soldiers (such as requests for leave and pay changes). Most PSCs and FAOs won't accept a personnel action unless it's forwarded on a UTL. The UTL verifies what documents you've forwarded. You or your first sergeant should review and sign all UTLs leaving your unit—the transmittal form is that important. Accuracy and timeliness are essential, if you care for your soldiers. Don't accumulate UTLs and send them as a group; send them to the FAO or PSC *daily*. A good inspection will locate problems in UTL preparation and transmission every time.

Personnel Management

Thoughtful personnel management characterizes all good commanders. Seven areas need your attention: ***Promotions, Sponsorship, Publications, Equal Opportunity, Non-Combatant Evacuation & Preparation for Overseas Movement, and Finance***. These programs are important because they affect your entire unit.

PROMOTIONS: Management of your promotion system must be *fair and known by every soldier in your unit*.

Any slip, in either factor, will cause more grief than you ever imagined.

War Story

A battalion commander visited one of his units and, as was his custom, had a RAP session with all the young enlisted soldiers (no NCOs). The only soldiers in the room were the young "Indians" and the battalion commander, the "Chief." The hottest issue brought to the battalion commander's attention was this unit's unfair promotion system, including complaints of favoritism, padding the numbers, and other horror stories. The battalion commander listened and told the troops he'd get back to them after he talked with their chain of command. He did just that; he checked the entire promotion process. He also had his battalion adjutant and personnel services NCO review promotion records for the last six months to ensure that criteria were being computed correctly. The investigation revealed the unit's promotion system was fair and all regulations were being followed. The problem was that the soldiers didn't understand the system, especially the mathematical computation for waivers. The unit had a fair system, but no one had explained it to the troops. That particular chain of command, from the unit commander to the squad leader, soon became the Army's foremost authorities on promotions for young soldiers. Remember, everyone must understand the system.

You must ensure all your soldiers appear before a promotion board (when they're eligible) as prepared as they can be. You must separate your truly good squad leaders and platoon sergeants from the rest of the pack. When you find a sergeant who sincerely helps his soldiers prepare for boards, he'll be one of the most respected sergeants in your unit.

Many battalions publish promotion guides for soldiers appearing before E5 and E6 boards. If your battalion does so, ensure the soldier's first-line supervisor uses that guide to prepare the soldier for the board.

Tip   **Ask the battalion CSM if you can sit in on a board proceeding. You'll find the boards are very fair and professionally run—not at all like the war stories you may hear from your soldiers.**

If your battalion doesn't have a promotion guide, talk with your battalion CSM and find out how boards are conducted. But if you have a good 1SG, you won't have to do that, because the 1SG normally is a member of the monthly promotion board. He can tell you, and your troops, what to know and how to prepare.

Tip   **Develop a unit policy that requires that a soldier's first-line supervisor be present at his promotion board. Word will soon get out that if a soldier isn't prepared, the first-line supervisor and the first sergeant can count on a meeting of the minds with the battalion CSM. Supervisors and 1SGs will make sure their troops are ready for the next board.**

Use your 1SG and battalion CSM to ensure your sergeants first class and above are ready for their centrally selected Department of the Army promotion boards. Many CSMs have been on these boards and could present their observations at a Non-Commissioned Officer development session.

When you don't recommend for promotion a specialist or lower-ranking soldier who satisfies the promotion criteria, counsel that soldier in writing. Tell her why you withheld your recommendation—what shortcomings you expect will be rectified. Follow the same procedure for soldiers not recommended by the battalion E5 and E6 board. **Put your remarks in writing!**

Don't forget your SIDPERS CO1 report. It lists, by name, all soldiers eligible for promotion to E2 through E4 with and without waivers. The CO1 report also will tell you how many soldiers you can promote with waivers. Make sure it's accurate.

SPONSORSHIP: Show me a company with an effective sponsorship program and I'll show you a unit that's probably good at everything it does. First impressions are lasting. It makes all the difference in the world how a soldier and his family are welcomed into a unit. You can put effort into a first-class sponsorship system or pay the price; the choice is yours. Here are some key ingredients to a good sponsorship program:

• Provide a detailed and personalized welcome letter and packet well in advance of arrival. Include sponsorship information for the spouse and family members, such as job information for the spouse and school information for the children.

• Assign sponsors to each new arrival.
  –Assign at same rank or greater.
  –Assign married to married and single to single.
  –Give the sponsor a checklist of duties.
  –Train the sponsor.
  –Give the sponsor time to do the sponsorship right.
  –Follow up on the sponsor's job.
  –Recognize good sponsors.

• Automate your sponsorship system as much as possible, but always send a hand-written additional note.

• In-processing is only *part* of your sponsorship program. Many commanders forget *out-processing* sponsorship. Don't!

If your unit doesn't have an effective sponsorship program, find out who does and copy it. Be sure your sponsorship program is tailored for your unit, especially if you're located overseas. A wise 1SG once said: "If the formal leaders of a unit don't take charge before a soldier reports in, the informal 'leaders' may . . . and those may not be the ones you want to influence new arrivals."

War Story

A second lieutenant, his wife, and their small child were assigned to Germany directly out of the officer's basic course. The sponsorship of this family was a disaster: No welcome letter, no assigned sponsor, no place to stay, and on and on. Perseverance on the lieutenant's part finally got the family settled, without help from the unit commander. The lieutenant didn't mention his sponsorship problems to the battalion commander at his initial interview; however, his wife wasn't so shy. At the first social function she attended, she "unloaded" to the battalion commander's wife. The next day, the company commander and battalion commander "talked." The real loss, though, was that the wife never forgot her initial experience with the Army. The lieutenant was a super officer, but because of his wife's distaste for the military, he left the Army at the end of his European tour.

PUBLICATIONS: How many times have you heard this comment at an inspection exit brief? "Publications UNSAT because. . . " Perhaps the comment continued with these phrases:

- Publications clerk untrained and not knowledgeable.
- Missing publications.
- Publications outdated or not updated.
- No internal distribution system for publications.
- DA 12 Series—nonexistent.

Yes, it's a fact that publications do not turn anyone on; yet, the value of current publications to the unit is immense. No one stops to think that your motor pool might be using outdated publications, until the motor pool fails an inspection because it's using obsolete regulations.

The key to success is having a *trained*, conscientious clerk who knows what she is doing. If you aren't that fortunate, tell your 1SG he has a "personal" problem he needs to correct. If you need help, go to the battalion S-1 office or your local MAIT. Or find another unit commander who has a good publications account and borrow his clerk for awhile. Whatever you do, find help early. In many instances, three to six months are needed to rectify publications problems. Start now!

The next time you're in the motor pool, select a piece of equipment and determine, by using DA Pam 25-30, *Consolidated Index of Army Publications and Blank Forms*, what the most current publications are for that piece of equipment. Ask a mechanic **Tip** **to provide you his copy of the publications in question. Are they current? Have they been used lately? Also, ask these soldiers how they request publications. If you get blank stares, you have another challenge to meet.**

EQUAL OPPORTUNITY (EO): Give your equal opportunity program lip service and you're asking for trouble. Let there be no doubt in anyone's mind—*you* are your unit's equal opportunity officer, appointed on orders. Conduct your required meetings, follow the regulations, and practice the following:

- Take action to prevent an incident *before* it happens.
- Publish your EO standards. Ensure your chain of command and soldiers *understand* your standards and the procedures for redressing complaints.
- Conduct EO classes to ensure everyone knows about your EO program.
- Use outside sources (chaplain, doctor, or battalion or higher EO officer) to help train newcomers and handle incidents. Request periodic staff visits, if necessary.
- Take *swift* and fair action on EO incidents, especially incidents involving racial or sexual harassment. Get your lawyer involved.

Your equal opportunity goal is to create a command climate that nurtures fair treatment for all soldiers.

Tip Shortly after you assume command, request the battalion or higher equal opportunity officer to conduct an EO effectiveness survey. This survey will identify potential EO problems in your unit. If you use the brigade EO representative, ensure that your boss knows before the survey.

NONCOMBATANT EVACUATION OPERATION (NEO) & PREPARATION FOR OVERSEAS MOVEMENT (POM): NEO concerns evacuating a soldier's family from overseas. POM concerns readying a soldier and his unit to leave CONUS and preparing his family for his departure. Both programs focus on the family.

Your role is to ensure proper planning and execution of these programs. The only way to do so is to ensure the updating of all processing, training, and testing, as required. Don't take shortcuts. Get the families involved, especially in the exercises. These preparations can be highly emotional and can affect your soldier's morale. Don't take lightly your responsibility to ensure soldiers, and their families, are prepared for combat.

FINANCE: A soldier with pay problems is a soldier who isn't thinking about his job. Ensure your chain of command is quick to help soldiers with pay difficulties. Too much is at stake, especially if the soldier has a family. Here are some ways to help:

- **CHAIN OF COMMAND REVIEWS OF MONTHLY LES**: Develop a system that requires you, your 1SG, your platoon leaders, your platoon sergeants (or any combination of the above) to review each soldier's monthly Leave and Earning Statement (LES). Carefully examine each for non- entitlement items, omitted entitlement items, and accrued leave data, specifically:

    — **Basic Allowance for Subsistence (BAS)**: If a soldier has a meal card, he shouldn't receive BAS. If a soldier has authorization to ration separately, he's entitled to BAS.

- —**Basic Allowance for Quarters (BAQ)**: If a soldie lives in military housing, he shouldn't receive BAQ. If a soldier doesn't live in military quarters he's entitled to BAQ.
- —**Pay grade**: Ensure the soldier's pay grade is correc on the LES. Promotion and reduction orders defi‐ nitely impact a soldier's pay.
- —**Leave data**: As discussed earlier, a review of leave data can help determine who needs leave and who's in the hole. Have your 1SG or platoon ser‐ geant keep a record of each soldier's accrued leave balance.
- —**Other items to look for**: Is the soldier in a "no-pay-due" status? Is the soldier in debt? Is the soldier on SURE–PAY?

Tip Your 1SG should be an expert on the LES. He should scan the statements when they arrive and give them to the platoon ser‐ geants to review in detail. Once the platoon sergeants have re‐ viewed the LESs, the 1SG should question them about the LESs of one or two soldiers in their platoon who had dis‐ crepancies noted during his review. This review method trains the platoon sergeants to become "experts" on the LES. Even‐ tually, the time spent on reviewing will decrease, but the review will remain a big service to the soldier and the government.

- **SURE-PAY**: Sure-pay isn't an option for any soldier who entered the military after 30 September 1985; it's man‐ datory. You should encourage soldiers who entered active duty before October 1985 to join the program. The soldier, his family, and the government all benefit.

War Story

A new company commander discovered her unit sure-pay participation was extremely low and she wanted to know why. She looked at a roster of nonparticipants and talked with each of them. Three-fourths had no reason for their lack of participation. No one had ever explained the

> *advantages for joining the program. Before long, her*
> *unit's sure-pay participation exceeded the Army's goal,*
> *after she had explained the benefits. Her subordinate*
> *chain of command saw the light, followed her example,*
> *and the participation rate for this unit remained high.*

- **UNIT TRANSMITTAL LETTER (UTL) SUBMIS-SION**: Heads-up financial support to your soldiers equates to prompt, accurate, daily submission of UTLs to the FAO. It's a must!

Let's go back to the beginning for a moment . . .

Remember four months after you took command and the late NCO-ERs your personnel sergeant told the chaplain about?
- After four months in command, should you have discovered the four late NCO-ERs?
- What's wrong with the NCO-ER processing system described?
- How will you correct this problem?
- How will you handle your first sergeant's incompetence?
- How extensive is the career damage to the four sergeants with NCO-ERs three months late?

Answer these questions in light of what you've read in this chapter. If you don't know the answers to these questions, you should know where to get the answers. Now do you see how important your personnel and administration responsibilities are?

The Bottom Line
for
Personnel and Administration

- YOUR PERSONNEL AND ADMINISTRATION RE-SPONSIBILITIES. Process personnel actions efficiently and establish effective personnel management programs.

- SIDPERS. Submit all reports accurately and timely.

- NCO-ER. Treat it as if it were your own.

- OER. The senior rater section separates the best from the rest.

- AWARDS. A definite "money-maker"—always go first class.

- REENLISTMENT. Reenlistment is a privilege. Spend *your* time on the winners.

- LEAVE. Use it and encourage your soldiers to use it.

- PROMOTION SYSTEM. Must be fair, published, and known by your soldiers.

- SPONSORSHIP PROGRAM. First impressions are lasting—don't drop your guard in this area.

- FINANCE. Prompt and aggressive support for a soldier with pay problems is a must.

Bibliography for Personnel and Administration

All Ranks Personnel Update

AR 600-38, *Meal Card Management.*

AR 623-105, *Officer Evaluation Reporting System.*

AR 623-205, *Enlisted Evaluation Reporting System.*

DA Pam 25-30, *Consolidated Index of Army Publications and Blank Forms.*

DA Pam 600-8, *Management and Administration Procedures.*

DA Pam 600-8-1, *SIDPERS Unit Level Procedures.*

DA Pam 600-8-20, *SIDPERS Handbook for Commanders.*

DA Pam 600-67, *Effective Writing for Army Leaders*
(This short pamphlet is must reading for your officers and NCOs.)

Enlisted Ranks Personnel Update.

Officers Ranks Personnel Update.

Personnel Evaluation Update.

TC 12-17, *Adjutant's Call, The S-1 Handbook.*

6. Training

Training is our top priority—it is the cornerstone of combat readiness.

Gen. Carl E. Vuono	John O. Marsh, Jr.
Army Chief of Staff	Secretary of the Army

THIS COULD HAPPEN TO YOU—Your mission is security for a NATO site in Germany. You're sharp, aggressive, mature. You stress training constantly, particularly because it's difficult to get quality training time. You spend months planning and developing a "leaders weekend"—your opportunity to spend quality time with your unit leadership and conduct good training. You spare no expense. You have aggressors, smoke, simulators, and Multiple Integrated Laser Engagement System (MILES) equipment. You have your planning sessions and map out exactly how you want the training to go. Because of the security requirements of your "real-world" mission, you decide that participants will carry live ammunition, as well as blank ammunition.

You conduct extensive safety briefings. All live ammunition will go in the cargo pockets of the battle dress uniform pants. Magazines with blanks go in the ammunition pouch and the weapon itself. All weapons will have blank adapters. You task all platoon sergeants to double-check their soldiers for strict compliance with your safety instructions. In fact, you assign one platoon sergeant to check everyone as he or she exits the building to ensure blank adapters are on all weapons. Anyone who sees an unsafe act is to call an immediate halt to the exercise by yelling "cease fire." You've thoroughly briefed everyone.

The morning training goes well. The After-Action Reviews (AARs) are comprehensive and very beneficial. Morale is high and everyone looks forward to the afternoon training session.

In the afternoon, however, disaster strikes. During a difficult and heated firefight between the aggressors and the defenders, one nervous buck sergeant becomes disoriented and inadvertently takes a magazine of live ammunition from his BDU pocket, locks, loads, and fires. He doesn't realize his blank adapter is missing. The end result is a bullet that kills a fellow soldier.

The AR 15-6 investigation indicates several mistakes occurred in the planning for the training, and some safety violations weren't reported.

WHAT DO YOU DO NOW, COMPANY COMMANDER?

The Company Commander's Training Responsibilities

Training to fight to win is your number-one priority. *Training always has been and always will be a commander's most important responsibility.*

★ ★ ★ ★ ★ *THE BRASS SAYS*

General Douglas MacArthur on training: In no other profession are the penalties for employing untrained personnel so appalling or so irrevocable as in the military.

General George C. Marshall on training: In the past, we have jeopardized our future, penalized our leaders, and sacrificed our men by training untrained troops on the battlefield.

General E. C. Meyer on training: The difference between a rabble and an effective professional Army is training. No task is more important than training.

General Carl Vuono on training: Our nation expects us to prepare its sons and daughters for battle. To lose one soldier because he or she wasn't properly trained is dereliction of duty.

The noun **TRAINING** is made up of three verbs: **TRAIN, TRAIN,** and **TRAIN**. This thought translates to **PLAN**, **EXECUTE**, and **ASSESS**. But you can't do all three by yourself. You need guidance from your battalion staff and input from your subordinate chain of command. It's a team effort focused on one objective: Training to fight to win. Insist on *quality* training and always train to a high *standard*. This is always *your* winning edge.

Educate Yourself

REVIEW REGULATIONS AND INSPECTION REPORTS: Using training regulations means immediate grasp of the concepts. So much has been written about training you might well wonder if anything is left to write about it. Your goal is to read until you understand the big picture and how you should grasp your company's participation in it. Review AR 350-1, *Army Training*, the 25-series Field Manuals, and Training Circulars, particularly in those areas you're least familiar with. Lieutenant General Arthur Collins' book, *Common Sense Training*, is *must* reading from cover to cover. Collins' book puts training in its proper perspective because he views it from the company commander's point of view.

Review your company's two most recent battalion inspection reports. Do common training deficiencies show up? Have all the recurring deficiencies been fixed? Compare these inspection reports with the last IG or command inspection. Are the training deficiencies similar? If so, you have a problem. After-action reports from unit exercises should help you determine training areas in which you can focus your efforts, especially at the beginning of your command tour.

TALK WITH KEY INDIVIDUALS: *Your battalion S-3 and operations NCO* are your two key people. They can tell you how your unit *actually* trains because, more than likely, the battalion S-3 has an inspection team that—announced or unannounced—checks your unit's training. It's smart to visit with them frequently. Ask their advice on your unit's strengths and weaknesses.

Constantly check the training in your company. If a squad leader is training his squad in the field for three days, make an _unannounced_ appearance at 2200 hours on his second night. You may be amazed at what you find. Ask squad members the FTX training objective, the squad's mission, and how this training will better prepare them for future operations. Ask squad members the last time they saw their platoon leader and platoon sergeant. If it's been a while, you have a problem. Ask the squad leader how he assesses the effectiveness of the training. Listen to his answers and see what's on the minds of the soldiers in his squad. If what you find that night pleasantly surprises you, be sure to say so and give the squad leader a pat on the back.

Tip

Your *battalion executive officer and command sergeant major* are prime sources of information about the battalion commander's training priorities. Get their guidance; it may save you a layer of your skin. The CSM periodically accompanies the battalion commander when he inspects your unit's training. He can give you tips on how to correct problems or alert you to future pitfalls. The executive officer's been in your shoes; he can recommend ways to fix particularly hard-to-solve training problems.

Your fellow *company commanders* also are excellent sources. Depending on their command tenure, they've probably gone through everything you're about to experience and can tell you how they'd do it again—given the opportunity. Ask them:

- What were your biggest training problems when you assumed command?
- What training programs best serve my soldiers?

- How do you eliminate training detractors?
- What are your greatest sources for training support?
- How involved do you get in training? Give me examples.
- What have been your most successful training initiatives?

Visit the *brigade training officer*. Discuss the brigade's mission and the training guidance issued by brigade to support that mission. How far in advance do they lock in the training schedule? How often do they send out their inspection team? Determine the most common mistakes unit commanders make in training and ask for examples of effective training programs.

Now, talk with *your battalion commander*. You've read *Common Sense Training*, reviewed regulations and inspection reports, talked with his staff and other commanders, and you know you can handle your number one priority—training. Listen intently to what the battalion commander says and before you leave his office, be sure you understand his views about training.

VISIT KEY ORGANIZATIONS: Visit your local *Learning Resource Center*. Many commanders neglect the Learning Resource Center, even though it can really help in individual training. The center has Training Extension Course (TEC) lessons, Soldier Training Programs (STPs), current regulations and manuals, and correspondence course assistance.

Use the Learning Resource Center and the Education Center (sometimes the same office) to develop special courses for squad and platoon elements in your unit. For example, these centers can give CPR (cardiopulmonary resuscitation) training to large groups, contract out Preventive Maintenance Checks and Services (PMCS) instruction, and arrange for college courses. Your imagination plus the centers' resources

Tip

can produce invaluable training on your turf and at the time you want it. Go with your unit officers and NCOs on a tour of the Learning Resource Center and Education Center. Consider including this orientation as a part of your Officer and Noncommissioned Officer Professional Development Programs.

Visit your local *range control*. You'll spend considerable time on all sorts of weapons ranges. Know what they offer, when they do it, and what your troops can expect each time they go there.

Develop a Training Philosophy

Never doubt that training is your number one priority. Adopt this training philosophy: EVERYTHING YOUR UNIT DOES IS TRAINING. Maintenance is training; ammunition accountability is training; administration is training; PT is training. You set the standards and you and your chain of command test how well they work.

★ ★ ★ ★ ★ *THE BRASS SAYS*

Lieutenant General Arthur Collins on training: Too many commanders are not aware that training is and should be related to everything a unit does—or can have happen to it.

Everyone in your unit should know your goal is to train in peace as you will fight in war. Base your training philosophy on your mission. Carefully analyze your mission; identify the tasks for your unit; make these tasks part of the training schedule. (More about training schedules later.) Every training task your soldiers perform should relate to your go-to-war mission. Here are some other items you should include in your training philosophy:

UNIT INTEGRITY—Maintain unit integrity for every assigned task. It builds teamwork, increases cohesion, and enhances proficiency. The more soldiers work together as a team, the greater the chance for mission success.

Guard duty is training—physical security training. If your unit must provide five guards for a particular guard duty, don't pull **Tip** five soldiers from different platoons. Send five soldiers from one platoon. Expand this example to any assigned task or training requirement. The key is to use the principle of unit integrity when you assign duties.

DECENTRALIZATION—Although you're responsible for your unit's training, you're not the primary trainer. Your sergeants are your primary trainers; therefore, let them do it. Give them the authority and responsibility they need. Training in a unit isn't done by committee. It's done by squad and platoon sergeants. Your job is to push training responsibility to the lowest level appropriate and then provide adequate support. Don't forget to give the trainer sufficient *time* to prepare for an exercise, whatever the required training. When you keep your training program decentralized, you strengthen the chain of command.

★ ★ ★ ★ ★ *THE BRASS SAYS*

Sergeant Major of the Army Julius W. Gates on delegation of training: Delegating the training responsibility down to the lowest level has its benefit. It fosters unity and confidence because the squad leader demonstrates that he knows how to do the task.

PERFORMANCE-ORIENTED TRAINING—Ensure your trainers use every available tool and technique to conduct hands-on training. Pure lecture training is a dud . . . period! If a soldier sees, hears, touches, tastes, and smells his or her training, the lesson lasts. You're after total involvement.

111

War Story

A squad leader had to conduct a PMCS class for his squad. He decided to short circuit the system and teach the class in a classroom. He used no slides, films, models . . . nothing. He simply "talked" for an hour. As luck would have it, the battalion command sergeant major decided to make an unannounced visit. The CSM not only "ate the squad leader's lunch" but those of the entire NCO chain of command for failing to review the squad leader's training plan. The CSM said, "There's absolutely no excuse for not teaching PMCS in the motor pool using the hands-on method. Anything short of that is wasting a soldier's valuable time."

REALISM—Realism is first cousin to performance-oriented training. Including as much reality in your training as possible makes sense, so long as you train with safety and common sense. Use noise simulators and smoke. "Kill" leaders at vital moments, so their subordinates have to take over. Let your imagination loose. Get away from your home base. Train in the field. Train in cold weather, at night, and for extended periods in poor weather. **Remember, fair-weather soldiers lose in combat.**

Tip Get your low-density MOS soldiers to the field. How many times has your key mechanic been pulled from training because something had to be repaired immediately? If that mechanic were an hour away in the field, your chain of command would solve the problem another way. Combine normal classroom training with the requirement to set up and disassemble your unit tactical operations center. *Tactically* proceed to the field, set up tents and other required items, conduct the classes, disassemble the tents, and *tactically* return to your headquarters. Now, that's BENEFICIAL TRAINING.

SAFETY—Preach training safety day and night. But don't be afraid to take acceptable risks to make your training realistic. What's an acceptable risk? There is no book solution. It's a risk you take, based on your common sense and ability to make an educated decision. If it's dumb, don't do it. If it's an acceptable risk, train on.

★ ★ ★ ★ ★ *THE BRASS SAYS*

Lieutenant General Henry Doctor, Jr, on training safety: Leaders must demand safety in training for two reasons. (1) It protects lives and equipment during training. (2) It trains our soldiers to practice safety on the battlefield. Safety does not inhibit mission accomplishment; it preserves our combat forces.

TRAINING DETRACTORS—Training detractors can be a unit's number one downfall. Use your captain's bars to eliminate such training detractors as these:

—Poor training area.
—Insufficient number of troops.
—Post details.
—Medical and dental appointments.
—Equipment shortages.
—Personnel actions.
—"Unsanitized" battalion taskings.

Training detractors will *always* be present. If a cat has nine lives, a training detractor has 100. Use your chain of command—both up and down. Your ingenuity and INITIATIVE can reduce or remove a detractor. If you can't kill the detractor, turn it into a training opportunity. Discuss with your chain of command how the detractor will hamper a particular exercise. Then get on with the mission.

Establish ground rules on "taskings" received from the battalion staff that you know will be training detractors. *Initially*, you may want to establish a policy that only you or your first sergeant can accept a tasking from the battalion staff. Don't allow your subordinates to accept taskings without your or your first sergeant's approval. This procedure will help you control detractors. Once you and the battalion staff are on the same wavelength, relax your approval authority.

Tip

A note of caution: Don't be lulled into thinking that training detractors are always "outside" influences on the unit. One of your biggest training detractors will be *your* trainers' lack of knowledge. The keys to success are twofold:

One, give your trainer the time, references, and material to properly prepare himself.

Two, have a supervisor check the trainer, certifying that the trainer really is ready to conduct the training.

Tip Use the "murder board" technique. Have your trainer present his training to one or more key unit leaders before his scheduled class or activity. This technique helps the trainer alleviate problems and ensures he knows what he is doing. If you conduct one or two tough murder boards, the word will spread quickly that trainers must have their acts together before appearing before the unit murder board. Who benefits? Your soldiers.

SUSTAINMENT TRAINING—Sustainment training, according to FM 25-3, *Training in Units*, is the repetitive execution of essential tasks throughout the unit training program. Your concern is to determine how frequently a particular task or battle drill needs to be taught to your soldiers. The frequency of teaching a task depends on how critical the task is and how well your soldiers remember that task. A weekly training meeting is an ideal time to discuss what subjects should receive sustainment training.

Incorporating sustainment training isn't easy because of a constant turnover of soldiers who have varying degrees of proficiency. Good management by your unit leadership and your unit training sergeant will help. Also consider these items when incorporating sustainment training:

—Integrate sustainment training into individual and unit training every chance you get.

—Avoid peaking. Peaking your training for a particular event will do more harm than good in the long run.

—Vary your sustainment training. Incorporate repetitive tasks into varied environments.

MULTI-ECHELON TRAINING—Multi-echelon training is training leaders and soldiers at various levels simultaneously to meet training requirements at several levels at once. The key to multi-echelon training is detailed and coordinated planning. (Don't forget after-action reviews for each level of training.)

How would you conduct multi-echelon training for a company defense? Try this:

—Formulate objectives and standards for each level (individual, squad, platoon, and company).

—Plan and coordinate what each level must do.

—Put individual soldiers (especially limited duty and incapacitated soldiers) to work on first aid procedures directed at casualties.

—Set squads to work on team battle drills (for example, manning defensive positions on alert).

—Set platoons to work on checking small things (for example, mastering fortification principles, like mines and booby traps).

—Make sure the company can train as a unit and defend its position against an aggressor attack.

Consequently, leaders and soldiers are training at their assigned levels of responsibility. Everyone has a job to do, particularly in combat. If the different "team levels" aren't proficient in their tasks, the unit will fail.

PUBLISH YOUR TRAINING PHILOSOPHY—After you publish your command philosophy (your overall *modus operandi*), publish your training philosophy. It will establish your guidelines for the number one priority in your unit. It's too important not to *publish*.

Training Management

HOW TO TRAIN—The Army has a wealth of material that tells you how to train for specific tasks. Your unit training NCO has copies of specific materials your trainers need. Your responsibility is to "paint the big picture" for your unit. You'll develop a solid training program if you thoroughly **PLAN** your training, **EXECUTE** as you planned, and **ASSESS** your strengths and weaknesses.

- **PLAN**—Poor planning produces poor performance. A good training plan is the foundation for effective and challenging training. Here are some key ingredients for effective planning:

—IDENTIFY REQUIREMENTS—Identifying requirements is a big first step. From your mission, identify your Mission Essential Task List (METL). Your METL specifies tasks critical to your wartime mission.

Tip

Don't formulate or revise your METL alone. Use your entire subordinate chain of command. *Your entire unit training program should revolve around your METL;* consequently, you want everyone to "buy into" the program from the start. Once you've formulated your METL, have battalion headquarters approve it.

As you identify your METL, determine your unit's *current* capability to accomplish each task and prioritize the tasks requiring the greatest training. Start training to meet those tasks first.

—DEVELOP A LONG-RANGE TRAINING PLAN— Your long-range training plan isn't as hard to develop as you might think. Your battalion already should have a long-range training plan and your unit should be included in that plan. The battalion plan will tell you the major exercise schedule, the range schedule, and other major requirements for your unit. Use the battalion long-range calendar as a base, and then add your requirements. For example, you may want to go to the field several times before a major field exercise. Thus, include "practice" field deployments in your plan.

The experts differ on the length of time for long-range calendars. A good length is about 18 months—give or take six months. The long-range calendar is just a guide; you'll need to be flexible. Events beyond your control will change your calendar; however, *without* a long-range plan, you have no direction. A long-range plan is *not* just paperwork: It's your life.

—DEVELOP A SHORT-RANGE TRAINING PLAN— Your short-range training plan develops *specific* training objectives derived from your long-range plan. While short-range training plans vary in length, they normally last for three to six months. Modify the short-range plan as necessary.

Closely coordinate your short-range training plan with your battalion headquarters. For example, when you're at the "lock- in" phase, you'll need final coordination for such items as ranges, ammunition, and support vehicles. FM 25-2, *Unit Training Management*, is a good reference for long- and short-range planning.

—TRAINING SCHEDULE—The unit training schedule locks in details for required training by listing who, what, where, when, and how. The training schedule and the duty roster put a soldier at a particular place at a particular time.

As a general rule, you *prepare* your weekly training schedule three weeks to three months in advance, and you *publish* the weekly training schedule three weeks in advance. *AVOID CHANGING YOUR TRAINING SCHEDULE ONCE IT'S PUBLISHED.* If you plan properly, training schedule changes will be minimal. Some of your most frequent changes will come from the training detractors discussed earlier. Your battalion and brigade headquarters will cause some training schedule changes. However, if they're doing their jobs correctly, any changes they dictate will be as a last resort. Be positive and flexible—use changes as a training opportunity for your leaders. It's good training for combat.

—WEEKLY TRAINING MEETING—The weekly training meeting is useful—even if some unit commanders don't use it that often. This meeting is your final coordination for ensuring everyone is prepared for training the following week. Your key subordinate chain of command leaders—including your dining facility manager, motor sergeant, and supply sergeant—should attend. It's your pre-execution check—to determine responsibility and accountability. What to do at your training meeting:

• *HAVE AN AGENDA*, and stick to it. Distribute it in advance, so your key leaders are prepared to discuss their responsibilities. Don't surprise them in public. *Limit* the agenda to training. Discuss other unit matters only when they affect training.

• *DISCUSS HIGHER HEADQUARTERS TRAINING NOTES*—If you schedule your meeting *after* the battalion commander has held his meeting, you can include in your meeting his topics or changes.

• *DISCUSS PAST, PRESENT, AND FUTURE TRAINING*—Don't restrict the agenda simply to the next week's training. Discuss the strengths and challenges of last week's training and look ahead a few weeks to ensure that long-lead requirements are on track.

• *DISCUSS AND ALLOCATE RESOURCES*—You can *identify* your requirements all you want, but if you can't *support* them, you can't train. Your long-range plan should identify resources that require a long lead time, such as reserving training areas, scheduling firing ranges, ordering ammunition, and so forth. Your short-range plan identifies resources requiring shorter lead times, such as medical support, training devices, training aids, fuel, and so forth.

Don't forget funding. Do you have the funds for your required training? Has the dining facility manager purchased the correct number of MREs for the second platoon's field problem next week? Have the motor sergeant and supply sergeant procured fuel coupons? These funding questions should surface at the training meeting.

• *PUBLISH MINUTES*—Publish simple, handwritten notes of the meeting. They become a reminder to all involved of their responsibilities.

• **EXECUTE**—Proper execution of training develops unit proficiency and ensures mission accomplishment. If you lay the proper foundation, implement your training philosophy, and plan wisely, you'll execute properly. Keep in mind these key actions:

— Maintain unit integrity—always.
— Push decentralization.
— Strive for realism. But . . . train *SAFELY*.
— Plan regularly, carefully, imaginatively—planning is the linchpin of execution.
— Make your training challenging.
— Check your training constantly.

• **ASSESS**—As important as good planning is, a thorough assessment is as vital after each training event. Good assessment includes three types of evaluation:

—AFTER ACTION REVIEW (AAR)—AAR is a review of training that allows participants to discuss how it went. It's *the* most beneficial training assessment—for the trainee and trainer.

—EVALUATION RESULTS—Evaluation results are the formal or informal outbriefs or written reports provided, normally, to the next higher commander. Here is where the unit *leadership* can review itself.

Tip Ask your lieutenants or your NCOs this simple question: "How would you summarize this for the Old Man?" It gets them thinking, reminds them of their responsibilities, and produces good feedback for you.

—PERSONAL OBSERVATION—Personal observation is an incomplete assessment method, because you can't observe all the training all the time. *But* there's no substitute for the impressions you get through your own eyes and ears.

While you should use all three assessment methods, the AAR is the most beneficial for all concerned. FM 25-100, *Training the Force*, lists key elements of formal and informal AARs:

119

- Conduct AARs in conjunction with the event at each echelon of command.
- Focus on battle tasks derived from METLs.
- Focus on individual leader and collective training objectives.
- Involve all training participants at each echelon.
- Make it a professional two-way discussion of what occurred—good and bad—and how to improve performance. (Note: The most effective assessments, and often the most brutally honest, come from the soldiers.)
- Link lessons learned to subsequent training.
- Document your findings.

FC 25-20, *A Leader's Guide to After Action Reviews*, is a good source for additional information on AARs. Most field circulars lose their currency. But this one's a gem. Find a copy and keep it. The AAR is as beneficial to the evaluated unit as the training itself. *Ensure* your trainers know how to conduct an AAR. Don't hesitate to make the evaluated unit conduct the task again. In fact, plan for remedial training.

LEVELS OF TRAINING—A good training program includes training for *individual* soldiers, training for the *unit* as a whole, and training for the unit's *leaders*. A good program is like a three-legged stool—very stable when the legs are solid, but quick to collapse if one leg goes bad.

- **INDIVIDUAL TRAINING**—Who's responsible for individual training? According to AR 350-1, "Noncommissioned officers are the principal trainers of individual soldiers." Now and then at a unit formation, remind your soldiers they *also* must contribute toward this training. Training is always a team effort.

War Story

A new company commander reviewed his unit's recent Skill Qualification Test (SQT) results and noticed that the platoon with the lowest average also had two soldiers with the lowest failing scores. He immediately summoned their platoon leader, platoon sergeant, and squad leader for a one-sided "discussion." He then dismissed the group without giving them a chance to explain. The platoon sergeant and squad leader found the first sergeant and told him what happened. Later that afternoon, the first sergeant told the company commander the other side of the story. Basically, the squad leader went out of his way to work with his entire squad to prepare them for the test. He came into the unit at night and on weekends to help his soldiers prepare. The two soldiers in question couldn't have cared less about the test and didn't take advantage of the squad leader's help. The 1SG also told the company commander that all the other soldiers in this squad passed the SQT with higher-than-average scores.

Suppose it was you who had blown up before you had the full story. How would you repair the damage? One way is to send word through the 1SG that everything's fine now that you have the facts. Then, at the right moment, go to your platoon leader, platoon sergeant, and squad leader and apologize. Tell them you got hot too quickly, you didn't have the whole story, and you know they're doing a good job. Admit your mistake, show you're reasonable, back your 1SG, and keep your strong emphasis on training. Of course, the easiest way to prevent this situation is to remember the axiom, "There are two sides to every story," before you fly off the handle.

Individual training is two-way. The soldier and his NCO leader must work as a team. The Army's basis for judging individual training is the Individual Training Evaluation Program (ITEP). ITEP consists of three elements: Common task testing (CTT), skill qualification test (SQT), and the commander's evaluation. Together, these three evaluation tools determine your soldier's proficiency in his particular job.

—*Common Task Testing (CTT)*—The Army develops about 17 hands-on common task tests given annually in units to evaluate soldiers on critical common tasks. These are *common* tasks, which aren't specific to any particular MOS. Key CTT actions:

- Test your leaders first—including *you* and your lieutenants.
- Make sure your trainers give the CTT properly.
- Provide immediate feedback via an AAR.
- Evaluate results to determine your training requirements. Be careful. If no company-wide deficiency trend is seen, you have no need for company- led training. Let the individual soldier and his squad leader correct his deficiency.
- Integrate CTT with other training. (Discussed below.)

—Skill Qualification Test (SQT)—SQTs, written tests administered annually to enlisted soldiers, focus on a soldier's proficiency in his particular MOS. While the CTT can be administered anytime, SQTs are given only during certain periods of the year (usually during a three-month window). Address the following when dealing with the SQT:

- Start preparing your soldiers *early*—not a month before the test. Good NCOs can easily make up a pre-test, based on the SQT notice, to help your soldiers prepare for their official SQT.
- Support your soldiers. Ensure that each one has a soldier's manual for his MOS, a common skills manual, and a copy of the SQT notice.
- Get the Learning Resource Center involved.
- Conduct formal and informal study sessions for your soldiers. Good NCOs will make these sessions relevant to the soldiers' skills.
- Evaluate results to determine your training requirements, particularly in your low-density MOSs.

—Commander's Evaluation—You can't assess individual training in your unit by simply reviewing training reports and statistics on your desk. Get out with your soldiers:

● Pick a few soldiers at random who had CTT on four items last week and test them yourself. Do they remember how to do the test?

● Get your supply clerk to explain what she learned three days after her low-density training. If the discussion only lasts five minutes, you both have problems.

● Ask to see a soldier's job book (if your unit uses job books). Quiz him on a training item from two weeks ago. If the job book's empty, his answer may be empty, too.

Integrate your individual training into unit or collective training, so you teach individual skills that support collective tasks. For example, individual map reading, safety, and chemical tasks are easily integrated into a platoon reconnaissance exercise.

● **UNIT TRAINING**—Who's responsible for unit training? Right again: You are! Your primary concern is *unit* training and how all other training relates to the unit. Therefore, look at your training program as a series of building blocks. The base block is individual training and the remainder of your building is unit training. If your individual training is weak, your unit training may crumble. Remember these three points:

(1) Soldiers fight as units—not as individuals.

(2) Soldiers practice individual skills so they can develop unit skills.

(3) **Teamwork** is the key to effective unit training.

Units can be trained in numerous ways. The list below gives you some ideas to choose from. Choose events best suited for your unit, its mission, and your leaders:

— Tactical Exercises Without Troops (TEWT).
— Map Exercises (MAPEX).
— Battle Simulations.
— Command Field Exercises (CFX).
— Command Post Exercises (CPX).
— Field Training Exercises (FTX).
— Situational Training Exercises (STX).
— Emergency Deployment Readiness Exercises (EDRE).

— Operational Readiness Test (ORT).
— Army Training and Evaluation Program (ARTEP).
(**NOTE**: ARTEPs are *training* exercises, not tests.)

The first five examples train your unit leaders and selected subordinates, ensuring your command-and-control network is effective. The last five exercises train your entire unit.

War Story

One company commander gave his platoon leader an operations order to tactically take his platoon to the field and train on four key platoon missions. The company commander then fully supported the lieutenant with what he needed for this training. The company commander brought his own aggressors and provided as much realism as possible. The first 42 hours belonged to the lieutenant, to conduct his training. During the last six hours of the training exercise, the company commander brought the battalion commander to watch the platoon perform two of the four tasks: Conduct a recon, and establish a perimeter defense. The lieutenant and the platoon sergeant knew, prior to leaving garrison, that the battalion commander likely would be there. The company commander's method showed careful planning and execution. The exercise measured the platoon's proficiency and increased its esprit de corps. The training went well, because the company commander had made training a unit effort. He knew that—and so did his battalion commander.

Your challenge will be to keep your unit proficient, even though you'll have a constant rotation of personnel. To meet that challenge, keep the following pointers in mind:

- Emphasize fundamentals.
- Vary the training.

- Keep the training short.
- Evaluate as you train (with after-action reviews).
- Stress teamwork and safety.

War Story

One company commander developed an excellent driver's training program as part of his unit training. He established driver training standards and ensured that only quality personnel were licensed. He knew that not every soldier can or should drive. His four-phased, unit driver training program became a model for his brigade. The highlights follow:

1. **Basic Driver Training**
   - *Formalized instruction including safety precautions.*
   - *Familiarization with maintenance forms and dispatch procedures.*
   - *PMCS hands-on training.*
   - *Written and PMCS hands-on test and issue of learner's permit.*
2. **Supervised Driving**
   - *Driver/trainee must drive for 30 days or complete 500 miles of incident-free driving with a qualified assistant driver.*
   - *On completion of the above, driver/trainee must pass a performance road test given by a certified instructor.*
3. **Refresher Training**
   - *All licensed drivers require an annual check ride by an appointed unit NCO.*
   - *All drivers attend annual training for winter driving and cold-weather operations.*
4. **Remedial Driver Training**
   - *Any soldier who has an accident, fails a check ride, abuses equipment, or persists in poor driving attends remedial driver training.*

> *The key to this company commander's driving program was a carefully planned and executed driving program which involved not just drivers, but the chain of command in the company.*

● **LEADER TRAINING**—If the trainer isn't trained, how can he train the soldier? You can train leaders both formally and informally. To a great degree, you control the informal process, but the Department of the Army (DA) controls most of the formal process. The formal process is primarily DA school allocations for your officers and NCOs. For example, the Basic Noncommissioned Officers' Course (BNCOC) and the Advanced Noncommissioned Officers' Course (ANCOC) are professional schools for NCOs. The Officers' Basic Course (OBC) and Officers' Advance Course (OAC) are professional schools for officers. Your responsibility is to prepare your junior officers and NCOs to attend these courses. Don't delay a soldier from attending a professional school for any reason short of war. You and your boss didn't get to your positions by missing a key professional school.

Examples of informal training include the Primary Leadership Development Course (PLDC), Motor Officer Courses, and chemical courses for officers and NCOs. Informal courses normally are shorter than professional schools and the only expense to you and your unit is the loss of an individual for a short period. However, you will reap long-term dividends.

A commander who cares for his soldiers will ensure they attend as many informal schools as his unit can possibly afford. Ensure your soldier receives sufficient notice when he'll attend a particular school. The last-minute "hey you" notice is a killer for the soldier and damages unit morale. A good first sergeant will handle PLDC preparation for you.

Tip Develop, where necessary, an order of merit list for attending informal schools. Reward your good soldiers. Let your soldiers know that only the best soldiers receive school allocations. Arbitrarily handing out school allocations lowers morale and makes the training seem like a punishment, instead of a reward.

Another aspect of the informal process is the Officer Professional Development (OPD) and Noncommissioned Officer Professional Development (NCOPD) instruction in your unit. Here are some key considerations:

— Create genuine OPD and NCOPD programs that are worthwhile. Go first class or don't go at all!
— Plan ahead for OPD and NCOPD sessions; make them challenging, varied, and useful.
— Ask officers and NCOs what they want for their unit professional development classes.
— Take time to schedule OPD and NCOPD classes.
— Use your imagination to create meaningful training for your trainers (such as computerized instruction and video casette recorders).
— Talk with other unit commanders and senior NCOs for advice.

Leader training would not be complete without discussing the Military Qualification Standards (MQS) system. The MQS system is the most dramatic and beneficial improvement to officer training in years. For the first time, this system *standardizes* officer training and creates an atmosphere of responsibility.

You have a twofold responsibility:

One, personally ensure you are proficient in your MQS III common and branch tasks and stay abreast of your professional reading program.

Two, ensure you properly train and *mentor* your lieutenants, so they complete their MQS II requirements.

127

You have tremendous latitude in how you implement MQS training and evaluation in your unit. Be a role model. Provide your lieutenants with guidance and time to train and develop themselves. Use MQS as a "framework" for unit training. Remember, the more proficient you and your lieutenants are, the better you will perform your unit's mission.

TRAINING TOOLS—Training tools run the gamut from hip-pocket training to simulators. They help you vary your training, while at the same time keeping training challenging. The following partial list of training tools can help you in this regard:

• **HIP-POCKET TRAINING**—Hip-pocket training is nothing more than your platoon sergeants and squad leaders preparing alternate training in advance to use during dead time. Slack time sometimes occurs in a training day, because of poor planning, lack of coordination, or even unexpected poor weather. For example, your troops are on the range to qualify with their M16s, but they have no ammunition. The supply sergeant mistakenly ordered the ammunition delivered at 1000 hours. It's now 0800. What do you do with your troops for the next two hours? You now have the perfect opportunity for hip-pocket training ("opportunity training" in FM 25-3). In this example, one platoon sergeant and a squad leader will work with their soldiers on four CTT items while they wait for the ammunition. Another platoon will work on nuclear, biological, and chemical (NBC) training. Good trainers always have alternate training material. Hip-pocket training can be the difference between a sharp, ready unit and a mediocre one. It prevents "Hurry Up . . . And Wait" in *your* unit. No sitting in the bleachers killing time when the battalion commander unexpectedly shows up!

War Story

One sharp company commander devised a comprehensive hip-pocket training book for her trainers. In it, she covered every conceivable training subject by task, condition, and standard. And she designed it to fit in the large BDU pants pocket. All the platoon sergeant or squad leader had to do was open the book, pick a subject, and start teaching. Sometimes, at the previous weekly training meeting, the company commander picked a specific subject for hip-pocket training. The hip-pocket book proved to be invaluable to hip-pocket training.

- **CONCURRENT TRAINING**—Concurrent training involves training your soldiers simultaneously on different tasks. This training differs from hip-pocket training in that concurrent training is always scheduled in advance. Let's use the previous firing range example. You'll have several firing orders because the range isn't large enough for all your soldiers to fire at one time. Consequently, while one platoon fires, one platoon can train on proper sight alignment and sight picture. Another platoon can serve as coaches and ammo bearers. A fourth platoon can train on call-for-fire procedures and a fifth platoon can train on camouflage techniques. All soldiers are gainfully employed, **simultaneously.**
- **DRILLS**—FM 25-3, *Training in Units*, puts it this way: "Drills are standard collective methods and techniques for executing a small-unit collective task (such as dismounting a vehicle under fire, emplacing a POL refueling station, or operating a crew-served weapon). Drills are the connecting link between individual and collective tasks. There is only one Armywide way to execute a given drill. Drills are trained repetitiously and instinctively to standard." Drills play a major training role, especially in combat arms training. But drill training is a gradual process. You must teach a drill following a logical process, such as this one:

—"War game" the drill. Talk and diagram the drill for the troops first. Use a sand table or any training aid to make your point.
—Practice the drill in slow motion. Walk through the drill until every soldier understands his responsibility.
—Practice the drill at a regular pace. Use all required equipment and train as you would implement this drill in wartime.

—Evaluate the drill. Get an outside observer to critique the drill.

—Sustain your drill proficiency. Practice makes perfect.

Once your crews, squads, and platoons are proficient at certain drills, implement the drill under varied and demanding conditions—night, poor weather, smoke, whatever. Challenge them by exposing them to a variety of combat and weather conditions.

• **SIMULATION TRAINING**—Take notice: Simulation training and training devices are the high-tech training trends of the future. Like it or not, the Army simply can't afford the ammunition, gas, and maintenance required for every training event. However, keep everything in perspective. Simulators and training devices *supplement* other training. When you do supplement your training, try to use the best state-of-the-art equipment. In many ways, your soldiers get more effective, controlled training using simulation because the feedback is immediate.

Tip Ask the Brigade S-3 about the latest state-of-the-art simulation training and how to get it for your unit.

The *smart* company commander will integrate simulation training into his training program.

• **TECHNICAL TAPES**—Tech tapes aren't used as much today as they once were. The computer and video age soon will replace them. In the meantime, however, use them when necessary. They're particularly useful for individual training. Your Learning Resource Center can help.

• **JOB BOOK**—Are job books in or out? It depends. Job books provide a good record for individual training requirements; however, they're a headache to maintain. Maintaining current data on soldier training accomplishments has been a problem for years. Your solution, however, is simple. If you're required to maintain job books, then ensure your trainers and soldiers maintain them according to regulations. In other words, if your boss says it's important, make sure your unit does it right.

- **CERTIFICATION COURSES AND DIAGNOSTIC TESTS**—These training tools normally are implemented at battalion and higher levels; however, you're required to prepare your soldiers for both. Certification courses teach soldiers skills specific to their current assignments. Diagnostic tests identify strengths and weaknesses you can use for matching the right soldier with the right job. If certification courses and diagnostic tests are available, use them; if they aren't available, consider setting up your own.

- **ADVENTURE TRAINING**—Adventure training is an excellent way to augment your training program. Examples of adventure training could be ski trips (in conjunction with winter survival skills training), white water rafting trips (in conjunction with water safety training), backpacking trips (in conjunction with mountain survival training), and rappelling down mountains or out of helicopters. Let your imagination be your guide, but don't forget safety. And be sure you maintain unit integrity; don't mix and match soldiers from various platoons. Adventure training increases morale and esprit de corps. It's fun, it's different, it's physically challenging, and it serves a training purpose.

- **CHECK. CHECK. CHECK**—Your company changes a lot in one year. So **CHECK** your training—continually!

Combat Training Vs. Combat Support and Combat Service Support Training

Does a combat soldier look at training differently than a combat support (CS) or combat service support (CSS) soldier? You bet he does. Training is a combat soldier's livelihood; it can determine whether he lives or dies.

On the other hand, CS and CSS soldiers also have jobs in time of war—such as repairing tanks, issuing equipment, typing orders, gathering intelligence, driving trucks, or enforcing the law. As Inspector General of the Army, Lieutenant General Henry L. Doctor, Jr., said of the mission of a CS or CSS unit: "Train to survive to support." When does the CS or CSS soldier qualify with his weapon, master the skill of establishing a defensive position, or defend himself in a hazardous chemical environment? You must integrate the training for these survival skills with his or her supporting job—one of the greatest challenges a CS or CSS commander faces.

The distinction between combat and combat support and combat service support is important to realize and important to take advantage of. CS, CSS, and combat commanders must seek each other out to take advantage of every joint training opportunity. Only then will combat soldiers know about the extremely difficult logistical problems involved in supporting a combat unit. Joint training among CS, CSS, and combat units is an excellent way to foster TEAMWORK.

Let's go back to the beginning for a moment . . .

Remember the training death?
- What mistakes happened during the planning session for the "leaders' weekend"?
- Should you have briefed someone in your next higher headquarters on your training plan, particularly on the simultaneous use of live and training ammunition?
- Did you consider your "real world" mission a training detractor?
- Did you push decentralization too far?
- Where did training realism stop and an unacceptable risk begin?
- Why weren't the safety violations surfaced at the morning AAR? Maybe the AAR was not as free and open as you thought. Are you approachable?
- Was safety really a primary consideration during the training? If so, why mix live and training ammunition?

- If you had to do it all over again, what would you do differently?

Answer these questions in light of what you've read in this chapter. If you don't know the answers to these questions, you should know where to find the answers.

★ ★ ★ ★ ★ *THE BRASS SAYS*

General Richard E. Cavazos on the importance of training: Training is not done in a sterile environment of cold calculating management. Training has to be rooted in deep ideals and beliefs—something worth dying for. The warmth of service to those beliefs—love of country, pride and belief in each other—yes, duty, honor, country—that's the warrior ethic.

The Bottom Line
for
Training

- TRAINING. Your number one priority. Assume everything your unit does is training.

- SAFETY. A primary consideration in every training event.

- PLANNING. Your most important step in the training process.

- UNIT TRAINING. Your responsibility.

- INDIVIDUAL TRAINING. An individual soldier and NCO responsibility.

- TRAINING LEADERS. If the leader isn't trained, how can he train your soldiers? Get involved—up to your eyebrows.

- PERFORMANCE-ORIENTED TRAINING. Stress it.

- TRAINING DETRACTORS. Kill training detractors instantly or use them to your advantage.

- TRAINING TOOLS. Use them all—training tools help challenge soldiers.

- AFTER ACTION REVIEW. Spare no effort to conduct beneficial, two-way AARs. Concentrate on bottom-up communication.

Bibliography for Training

AR 350-1, *Army Training*.

Collins, Jr. Arthur S. *Common Sense Training*. San Francisco: Presidio Press, 1981.

FC 25-20, *A Leader's Guide to After Action Reviews*.

FM 25-2, *Unit Training Management*.

FM 25-3, *Training in Units*.

FM 25-100, *Training the Force*.

7. Supply

I don't know much about this thing called logistics: All I
know is that I want some.

Expression, famous since World War I,
attributed to various American generals

THIS COULD HAPPEN TO YOU—As a company commander, you're responsible and accountable for all
equipment issued to your unit. Your property accountability procedures haven't been the highlight of your command
tour, but you're working hard to fix the problems. Your company is in the middle of a major Modification Table of Organization and Equipment (MTO&E) transition. You and your
supply section are swamped with turn-in of excess and unserviceable equipment. Your challenge is further compli-
cated by unwieldy turn-in procedures. For example, your
third platoon, located 45 minutes from your headquarters,
will turn in unserviceable tents tomorrow. The platoon will
take the tents to the supply and service (S&S) company, approximately an hour north. The S&S company will inspect
the tents and verify their unserviceability. Then the platoon
will return the coded-out tents to platoon headquarters and
dispose of them. Then the platoon leader will take all the paperwork to another location in town to have the verification
accountability recorded. Finally, he'll forward the paperwork to your headquarters.

Your platoon leader calls you the next day. He tells you
that while he and his platoon sergeant were disposing of the
tents, a truck from the battalion operations section pulled
up and the new battalion training officer got out. The training officer had just completed his company command tour
and was (among other things) one general purpose small

tent short on his change-of-command inventory. He wanted your platoon leader to give him one of the coded-out tents to cover the shortage. The training officer told your platoon leader no harm would be done, since the tents were being destroyed anyway, and it would save the training officer a $763.98 deduction out of his next paycheck. Your platoon leader knows you and the training officer are old friends and wants to know what he should do.

What do you tell him, COMPANY COMMANDER? Before making your decision, you must fully understand your responsibility in property accountability. You're the "keeper of the keys" for a great deal of US Government property.

The Company Commander's Supply Responsibilities

You have two major supply roles—you're **RESPONSIBLE** for all unit property; and you're **ACCOUNTABLE** for ensuring all unit property is in working order and is properly documented on unit records.

RESPONSIBLE FOR ALL UNIT PROPERTY: As the responsible person, you must properly maintain, secure, and account for your unit property on unit records. You can't delegate your command responsibility. Even when others have hand receipts for unit property, you're not relieved of your responsibility for accountability.

AR 710-2, *Supply Policy Below The Wholesale Level*, requires a Command Supply Discipline Program (CSDP). This program provides a framework for organizing all your supply procedures. Learn about the CSDP before you take command.

ACCOUNTABLE FOR ALL UNIT PROPERTY: Accountability means that you must document your supplies and equipment in a formal record-keeping system, such as hand receipts. But everyone in your unit is responsible for property, not just the individual signed for an item of equipment. Stress this fact! Soldiers are less likely to damage or lose government property if they know *they're* responsible for its care. Literally, you may be "indebted" to Uncle Sam at the end of your tour if you neglect property accountability. More importantly, inattention to property may degrade your unit's combat readiness. It could well become another detractor that will "kill" your training.

★ ★ ★ ★ ★ *THE BRASS SAYS*

General Frederick J. Kroesen on the importance of supply: I think a company commander . . . should have a supply and maintenance program equal in *quality* to his training program. . . . He has to have respect for his property and equipment and develop that same respect in his men.

Educate Yourself

REVIEW REGULATIONS AND INSPECTION REPORTS: Make yourself as knowledgeable as possible about supply procedures. Start by scanning general Army Regulations and Field Manuals covering supply topics, especially the latest *Unit Supply Update*. You won't have time to read all these documents from cover to cover, however. Your most helpful document is TC 710-5, *Unit Commander's Supply Handbook*. It's designed specifically for you, the unit commander, and will quickly make you "supply smart."

After you have a general working knowledge of supply procedures, review the last two or three battalion supply inspection reports, the last IG report, and your unit's last Material Assistance and Inspection Team (MAIT) report. If possible, review these reports and regulations prior to assuming command, or before doing your change-of-command inventory. These documents usually paint an accurate picture of the unit's property accountability situation. You should especially look for recurring deficiencies, and *list them*. During your change- of-command inventory, see if the recurring deficiencies are fixed. If they aren't "fixed," correct them immediately after you assume command.

Tip A good indication of the quality of your supply officer and supply sergeant is whether they've corrected recurring deficiencies *before you arrive*. If you don't have good supply personnel, one of your first jobs will be to ensure they receive training.

TALK WITH KEY INDIVIDUALS: Talk with the *battalion Supply Officer* (S-4) and the *battalion Property Book Officer* (PBO). The S-4 probably prepared the last battalion supply inspection report. He'll know the strengths and weaknesses of your supply room personnel. Not only that, he can compare your operation with other units in the battalion.

The PBO answers your supply questions and gives you guidance on the proper way to conduct a change-of-command inventory. The jobs of the PBO and battalion S-4 are to support you. Doing poorly on an IG inspection in property accountability reflects on them **and** you.

Your *fellow company commanders* are still good sources of information. Seek their advice on the dos and don'ts of property accountability:

- What were your biggest supply problems when you assumed command?
- What advice do you have for me concerning the change-of- command inventory?
- What are the "Old Man's" key supply concerns?
- Where can you get the best property accountability assistance?
- How did you develop your command supply discipline program?

Now talk with your *battalion commander* about property accountability during your initial discussion with him. Make sure that when you leave the battalion commander's office you know his supply expectations.

VISIT KEY ORGANIZATIONS: Visit your *supply support activity* (SSA) where you order supplies and equipment. Talk with the SSA commander and ask for a tour of his facility so you can learn how his organization works. He can tell you what pitfalls to avoid when you order supplies and equipment.

Tip

Visit the SSA commander periodically. Ensure your unit requisitions and picks up supplies and equipment promptly. Discuss the length of time it takes the SSA to fill your class II, IV, and IX requisitions. Also, the SSA commander can help you get a particular item of equipment or a scarce supply item on short notice. Don't go to the well too often; but, in a severe drought, you want to know a well is nearby.

Visit your local *MAIT* or its equivalent. When members of this team say they're an assistance team, they're absolutely correct. Ask for the most common problems in property accountability and the MAIT's recommended solution. The MAIT also is a good source for logistics documents. Don't ask for a courtesy inspection right away: If you really need one, you need to coordinate that decision with your battalion headquarters. The battalion headquarters will more than likely request a MAIT inspection for the entire battalion. An excellent time for a MAIT inspection is six months before an annual general inspection. If it's not on your calendar, you ought to put it on.

If you educate yourself on your roles and responsibilities, you can establish a sound command supply discipline program. Remember that you can't do everything yourself. So educate your subordinates and soldiers that strict property responsibility is crucial to combat readiness.

Educate Your Unit on Supply Procedures

SET THE EXAMPLE: Setting the example is the best way to educate your unit. Send a signal by personally handling key property accountability issues, such as inventories or spot inspections of hand receipts. Ask tough questions, provide accurate solutions to accountability problems, and inspect at a level sufficient to pass any higher headquarter's inspection. Your knowledge of property accountability will help you gain the respect of your supply personnel and make your job a lot easier.

You probably have a lieutenant as your supply officer. Involve him
Tip *heavily* **in the education process. Push him hard to become an "expert" on supply procedures. He'll be a better commander later and will keep your supply room in good shape.**

SCHEDULE A MAIT VISIT: MAIT visits are the second best way to educate your unit. (Remember, don't schedule a MAIT visit unless your battalion headquarters approves your request.) The MAIT examines every logistical area in your unit and recommends solutions to problems. When the MAIT visits your unit, make sure all your soldiers are present. The greater the unit's participation, the greater its opportunity to improve property accountability. Lack of participation simply wastes the team's time.

CONDUCT UNIT CLASSES: Even though unit training time is crowded, classes on supply (for example, hand receipts and the proper care of equipment) should be an integral part of your training program. If you don't have well-maintained equipment, you can't train properly.

CONDUCT LOW-DENSITY TRAINING CLASSES: Low-density MOS personnel (such as supply personnel, cooks, mechanics, and clerks) often are the least-trained soldiers in your unit. But a supply clerk needs more supply education than his on-the-job training if he's to become proficient in his MOS. Make sure your soldiers have solid proficiency training.

Set aside half a day each week for low-density MOS soldiers to receive training in their primary MOS. This training *may*
Tip **involve closing some of your administrative and support offices a few hours per week. Make these closings part of the company's routine, so soldiers know when support services are curtailed.**

MONEY TALKS: At times you may have to use money as an accountability training tool. Establish your policy early: If you lose it, or destroy it, or damage it . . . *you pay for it!*

To maintain your unit's combat readiness and ensure you don't have to "buy" the unit on your departure, master your most important supply responsibilities. Let's start with some basic responsibilities.

Inventories

An inventory is a count of all supplies and equipment in a unit. It ensures quantities listed on property records agree with quantities on hand and the property is located where it should be. Here are a few of the inventories you'll probably conduct:

- Change of responsible officer inventory (commonly referred to as change-of-command inventory).
- Annual responsible officer inventory.
- Cyclic inventory (commonly referred to as monthly 10–percent inventory).
- Change of property book officer inventory.
- Command-directed inventory.
- Sensitive item inventory.
- Organizational clothing and individual equipment(OCIE) inventory.

The Army also differentiates *event-driven* inventories (such as the change of responsible officer inventory) from *time-driven* inventories (such as the cyclic inventory).

AR 710-2, DA Pam 710-2-1, *Using Unit Supply System, Manual Procedures*, and AR 735-5, *Policies and Procedures for Property Accountability*, are absolutely necessary for inventories and for most supply transactions at the unit level. Review in detail the chapters on inventories before starting any property survey. The **change-of-command** inventory, the **10-percent** inventory, and the **sensitive item** inventory are of particular concern to you:

CHANGE-OF-COMMAND INVENTORY: The change-of-command inventory is the most important inventory you'll conduct as a company commander. It sets the stage for all future supply operations. If you don't complete your initial change-of-command inventory correctly, you'll have property accountability problems throughout your assignment, and you may owe Uncle Sam "big bucks" when you leave. A thorough, fair change-of-command inventory also tells the rest of the unit that you view your property accountability responsibilities seriously. Change-of-command inventories are time-consuming and tedious. If you are satisfied with shortcuts, it could "cost" you dearly.

War Story

One gullible company commander didn't know a thing about change-of-command inventories and didn't do any research before his inventory. He took everyone's word that a piece of equipment was on hand. He didn't demand to see the items. Consequently, he finished his inventory in a scant few days. During his tour, he failed two battalion supply inspections (under two different battalion commanders) and was unfortunate enough to have two incompetent supply sergeants. Nevertheless, he remained personally accountable for all unit property. His replacement, 18 months later, was a smart, diligent captain who knew all about change-of-command inventories. The outgoing, gullible company commander ended his tour owing Uncle Sam $55,000—that's right, $55,000. Beyond the commander's personal loss, just imagine what his unit's combat readiness must have been during that 18-month period!

AR 710-2 says, "Thirty days will be allowed to accomplish the inventory." Don't rush. You may be *tempted* to see to lingering responsibilities at your old job. Resist this temptation. A proper inventory takes time and attention *before* you take over the reins of command. And if you need more time, ask for an extension, in *writing*, from your battalion commander before the 30-day period ends. Lieutenant General Andrew P. Chambers, former VII Corps Commander, felt so strongly about incoming commanders having sufficient time to conduct their change-of-command inventory that he sent a letter to his subordinate commanders, saying, "Only the most extreme circumstances should prevent a new commander from accomplishing his inventory prior to the change of command." Every commander in the corps knew what General Chambers thought about the issue and how he wanted it handled.

A change-of-command inventory has three phases: preparation, execution, and follow-up. Each phase has specific tasks you should complete "by the numbers" before going on to the next step. Here are some specific actions to take during each phase of the inventory:

PREPARATORY PHASE: During the preparatory phase, develop your strategy for the inventory.

Talk with your battalion commander.
- He should give you and the outgoing commander a detailed letter of instruction with expectations and procedures he wants followed.
- Get his concurrence for a 30-day inventory period before the change of command.
- Identify any particular problem areas you should examine closely.

Talk with the battalion S-4 and Property Book Officer.
- Get their advice on how to conduct the inventory.
- Ask about problems you should know about before the inventory.

Talk with your fellow company commanders.
- Get their advice and recommendations.
- Ask about problems they encountered with their inventories.

Read current reference materials.
- Modification Table of Organization and Equipment/Division Logistics System (MTOE/DLOGS).

- AR 710-2.
- AR 735-5.
- DA Pam 710-2-1.
- DA Pam 25-30, *Consolidated Index to Administrative Publications and Blank Forms* (to ensure all reference material is current—very important!).
- Local SOPs or policy letters.

Determine what to inventory. Conduct 100–percent inventory of all:

- Equipment and component parts.
- Installation and station property.
- Organizational property, clothing, and individual equipment.
- Housing property.

Develop your inventory strategy.

- Base your strategy on the above references and discussions.
- Make sure you're thorough and comfortable with your strategy.

Meet with the outgoing commander.

- State your strategy.
- Develop a joint inventory schedule.
- Resolve any problems.
- Be cordial, open, and clear.
- Don't be intimidated.

Tip

If the outgoing commander is *proficient*, he's already conducted a special pre-inventory to ensure all *his* property is accounted for and sub-hand receipts are current. He should give you a tentative inventory schedule. At the appointed inventory time, he should ensure all equipment is displayed properly and all required personnel are present. Be on the alert: Outgoing commander proficiency in this area is the exception rather than the rule.

INVENTORY PHASE: If you have a solid strategy, the inventory phase will be tedious, but productive.

- Publish a schedule and stick to it.

- See and count every piece of equipment and component part for which you're accountable.
- Take the supply sergeant with you during the inventory.
  —Ensure he or she has all reference material (such as hand receipts and component lists).
  —Reconcile *all* temporary hand receipts.
- Inventory all like items at the same time. (Don't give anyone time to shuffle missing items from one platoon or unit to another.) If you suspect such a problem, randomly pick three or four expensive pieces of equipment and go back a week later and, unannounced, re-inventory.
- Reconcile daily.
  —Report all overages and shortages to the outgoing commander.
  —Give him or her as much lead time as possible to rectify the situation.
  —Don't assume anything.

Tip If you're concerned about being unreasonable during an inventory, ask yourself this question: Will your successor accept the explanations you're hearing for the missing item? Remember, the *outgoing* commander is responsible for having all of his or her property in place and in order.

FOLLOW-UP PHASE: The follow-up phase is as important as the preparatory phase. All discrepancies should be resolved here.

- Verify all supply documentation.
- Prepare documentation for overages and shortages.
  —Statement of charges.
  —Cash collection vouchers.
  —Cash sales.
  —Reports of survey.
- Verify all unit property is properly hand receipted.
- Prepare an after-action report.

- Brief the after-action report to the battalion commander. Ensure the outgoing commander is present.
- Accept responsibility for the property by signing the unit property book or printout when you and the battalion commander are satisfied with the inventory.

The follow-up phase and its findings shouldn't come as a surprise to anyone, especially the outgoing commander. If you've provided a daily reconciliation he or she will have time to resolve any differences. Be considerate; 18 months from now the roles will be reversed. Treat your predecessor as you want to be treated when you change command—be firm but fair.

War Story

A battalion commander briefed the outgoing and incoming company commanders on their mutual change-of-command inventory responsibilities. One particular point the battalion commander stressed was the incoming commander must keep the outgoing commander totally informed (daily, if necessary), especially of any shortages, so the outgoing commander would have time to locate any missing property. The battalion commander didn't want anyone surprised. Contrary to the battalion commander's written and verbal instructions, the incoming commander didn't keep everyone informed. Instead, he completed the inventory, then told the outgoing commander that approximately $10,000 worth of equipment was missing. The outgoing commander was in shock and the battalion commander was irate. In the next three days, the outgoing commander located all but $56 worth of misplaced equipment. In the meantime, the incoming commander spent 30 minutes in the battalion commander's office . . . 30 long minutes. The lesson is really simple: Keep the lines of communication—formal and informal—open with your boss and the outgoing commander as you do a change-of-command inventory.

Remember, if change-of-command inventories are done right, future inventories will be based on accurate totals.

And save all your documentation; it will help you during other required inventories.

CYCLIC OR MONTHLY 10-PERCENT INVENTORY: Conduct this cyclic inventory monthly, quarterly, or semiannually. If you choose monthly, check 10 percent of your equipment; quarterly, check 25 percent of your equipment; semiannually, check 50 percent of your equipment.

As unit property book officer, you decide when to conduct your cyclic inventory; however, almost every Army document or former company commander recommends a monthly inventory. Such a procedure forces you to attend to property accountability matters more frequently, keeps your hand-receipt holders on their toes, and provides a 120-percent inventory of your equipment annually. Sometimes, your battalion commander may direct what items to check; on other items, you're on your own.

Tip Develop a schedule that tells all unit personnel which items of equipment you'll inventory each month. Hand receipt holders then can get the equipment ready for your inventory. Put the 10 percent inventory schedule on your training schedule, so your battalion commander and his staff know what you're up to. Look at DA Pam 710-2-1 if you want to know more about the 10-percent inventory.

SENSITIVE ITEM INVENTORY: Inventory all sensitive items (such as weapons, ammunition, and hazardous materials) monthly. The Army Master Data File lists all the sensitive items you'd ever want to meet. You or the hand receipt holders can do the inventory. If you don't conduct the inventory, you must sign a DF that certifies that the responsible individuals took care of it. If you conduct this inventory, do it at the same time you do your 10–percent monthly inventory. DA Pam 710-2-1 also covers the sensitive item inventory.

Tip

**Inventory all sensitive items used during alerts, maneu-
vers, and field problems immediately after the exercise.
Make sure no one goes home until sensitive items are
cleaned and accounted for.**

Property Records

The mere mention of the words "property records"
sends shivers through the bodies of courageous men and
women. The words evoke thoughts of a computer run
amuck, spewing records and forms throughout the army.
Take heart! Your supply officer and supply sergeant can handle the property records monster. Let them. You need only a
good idea of how these records work, where the property is,
and who's accountable if the property isn't where it's sup-
posed to be.

PROPERTY BOOK: The property book is the *official* record. Handle it carefully; always store it in a secure place.

Organization and installation property appear separately in the property book or in two separate books. If you
command a separate company, you'll normally have a manual property book. If you command a company in a division,
you'll normally have an automated property book system,
with a computer printout of your property that you periodically reconcile with your hand receipts. Check your property book or printout monthly for accurate accountability:

- Do equipment quantities match hand receipts?
- Are posted gains and losses documented with a
  voucher or other document?
- Do priority requests have proper approval?

War Story

One unfortunate commander had her manual property book "removed." No one caught the thief and no one found the property book. Finally, after three 100-percent inventories, a separate 100-percent inventory by a disinterested group of officers, and 15 months of total disruption, the unit returned to normal. Safeguard your property books!

HAND RECEIPTS: Hand receipts establish direct responsibility. A soldier who signs a hand receipt is responsible for that item. Sub-hand receipt all your unit property, from M-16s to watches. The normal procedure is to sub-hand receipt to the supervisor, who then sub-hand receipts to the user. Update your hand receipts every six months. Let your supply sergeant handle this chore.

★ ★ ★ ★ ★ *THE BRASS SAYS*

Lieutenant General Jimmy Ross on property accountability: Property accountability is vital. A commander must ensure that his property is hand-receipted to the lowest level. It's the commander's property—if he doesn't ensure it's properly hand receipted—who will?

WEAPONS RECORDS: Weapons are among your most important and visible property items. Their accountability can't be overstated, especially when such items are readily marketable to "units" outside the US Army. Your property book lists weapons by serial numbers.

Sub-hand receipt all weapons to your unit armorer. Ensure no soldier in your unit can draw a weapon from the arms room unless he or she follows strict procedures you've set up. Make sure a soldier signs a control sheet or arms room log for the weapon. Or, have him or her surrender their

DA Form 3749 *(Equipment Receipt)*, which assigns a specific weapon by serial number to a soldier. The procedure is simple and efficient. Soldiers who take shortcuts cause problems. Check your arms room accountability procedures frequently.

Tip
The absence of the unit armorer creates major problems. Make sure you always have a well-trained backup who fully knows what he's doing. You can't train someone "overnight" if your armorer goes on emergency leave.

Adjustment of Property Records

Prepare adjustment documents when government property is damaged, lost, or destroyed. These documents relieve you of property responsibility or help determine negligence. If your property book says you have five filing cabinets, but you only have four, prepare an adjustment form (as the case may dictate), so you don't have to pay for the missing filing cabinet. Look at AR 735-5 for more details. If you must investigate a suspected case of negligence or willful destruction, consult your lawyer and your battalion S-4.

Tip
Anyone who willfully or negligently damages, destroys, or loses government property pays for that property out of his or her paycheck. It's the law. Establish your standard early.

Here are four of the more common property record adjustment procedures:

CASH PAYMENT: When a soldier loses a hand tool or a piece of his organizational clothing and individual equipment (OCIE), he'll probably make a cash payment adjustment. If the soldier admits he was negligent and wants to resolve the situation easily, give him written authorization to purchase (cash only) a replacement hand tool from the self-service supply center (SSSC) or the item of clothing from the central issue facility (CIF). Depreciate the item by 10 percent if it wasn't new. Remember: the newly purchased item becomes the property of the US Government.

Tip Periodically conduct a full field layout of OCIE. Conduct these inspections quarterly, or after major field exercises. You'll probably find several missing OCIE items. Offer the soldier the opportunity to replace the missing item. Normally, a sharp platoon leader or platoon sergeant has handled the matter, or a 3x5 card will be in place of the missing item, stating, "I want to replace this item, please give me your written authorization so I can get my 10 percent discount." Soldiers usually replace small lost or damaged items without a problem.

CASH COLLECTION VOUCHER: When a soldier loses, damages, or destroys an item not currently available, use a cash collection voucher. If a soldier wants to pay for the missing item, complete DD Form 1131, *Cash Collection Voucher* (see AR 735-5), and send it to the local Finance Office with the *cash* payment. Since the amount of depreciation will vary, look at AR 735-5 for guidance. Ensure your supply sergeant does all the necessary paperwork and removes the item listed on the DD Form 1131 from your property records. One problem, though, is you can't use a cash collection voucher if the value of the lost item is *greater than the soldier's monthly base pay.*

STATEMENT OF CHARGES: Use a statement of charges when a soldier doesn't have the cash to pay for the equipment. This property adjustment permits payment to be deducted from a soldier's pay. You'll need a DD Form 362 (*Statement of Charges for Government Property Lost, Damaged, or Destroyed*) instead of a DD Form 1131.

While you want to be "hard-nosed" about property adjustment, don't forget your compassion either. A little known line in AR 735-5 reads: "If the charges exceed two-thirds of the person's monthly base pay, the unit commander will attach a letter to the statement of charges requesting the charges be prorated over a two month period or longer." In the interest of your troops, please take advantage of this provision.

Tip

The cash payment, cash collection voucher, and statement of charges adjustments have several characteristics in common:

- All transactions must be voluntary.
- Transactions can't exceed a soldier's monthly base pay.
- They can only be used for official purposes. Personal purchase isn't authorized.
- The Government retains ownership of all items. If the lost item is recovered, the soldier turns it into the supply room and submits a claim for reimbursement.
- Sensitive items can't be processed using these voluntary reimbursement methods. Instead, you must initiate a report of survey.

REPORT OF SURVEY: Use report of survey adjustment when you suspect negligence the soldier hasn't admitted to. AR 735-5 and FM 10-14-3, *Surveying Officer's Guide*, discuss the mechanics of how to do a report of survey. Here are some other suggestions:

- Think before you act. Have you considered other alternatives to resolve the situation? Reports of Survey are very costly.
- Stick to the time limit. You have 15 calendar days to initiate the survey after discovery of the damage, loss, or destruction.
- Adjust your property records after the survey.
- Take responsibility for surveys assigned to your lieutenants. Mentor them. Remember, their senior rater, your boss, is the appointing authority.

- Allow your lieutenants time to do surveys. Make it their primary duty and help them get legal advice, if necessary.
- Be inquisitive and thorough when reviewing reports of survey.

Tip Apply the following rule to reports of survey—do unto others as was probably *not* done unto you. Reports of survey efficiency will improve.

EXCESS PROPERTY: Don't horde your excess property! Company commanders tend to stockpile all the excess property they can hide with the idea they can use it to repay debts they owe to other units.

Any Inspector General will tell you excess property circumvents the supply system and does nothing but get a company commander in trouble. What do you do when the IG asks you where you store your excess property? Do you "compromise" and tell him you don't have any? Be careful, because the IG supply inspector (E7/8) just asked your supply clerk the same question and the clerk spilled his guts. Turn in excess property to your supply support activity and save yourself unnecessary heartburn.

War Story

A company commander inherited a unit that literally had three full rooms of excess equipment and furniture, some of which had been in the unit at least five years. Thinking he might need the excess, the company commander kept the equipment. However, the rooms belonged to another unit, so when his company was inspected, the excess was never found. One day, about six months after the company commander assumed command, the battalion commander paid him a special visit. The battalion commander showed him an anonymous letter from a

> *disgruntled soldier whom the company commander had just chaptered out of the Army. The letter revealed, among other things, the location of three full rooms of excess property belonging to his former company commander. Things went down hill from there. The company commander and his supply officer and supply sergeant took 10 full months to properly turn in all the excess equipment.*

If you don't need or use a piece of equipment, get rid of it—*legally*. Turn in unused equipment periodically and avoid time-consuming drills imposed by the above chain of command.

Your Budget

I can't even balance my checkbook. . . . How do I handle the company budget? Read on. Sometimes your battalion will manage your budget for you, but sometimes you're in charge of guarding the bank.

If at all possible, you should take control of your budget. If you hold the purse strings, you'll have more flexibility and a stronger sense of where government dollars go. That doesn't mean you won't have others doing the day-to-day accounting, however.

Usually, the supply officer also is the unit budget officer. But don't make the mistake of giving the good lieutenant a blank checkbook without rules to follow. The following financial management suggestions should help you both stay out of jail:

- **Develop a yearly budget plan.**
    —Start by comparing last year's plan with last year's actual costs.
    —Get input from your platoons and support sections and make them justify their requests. What are their actual needs? What are their real priorities? How much does it cost to move your unit one mile?

Based on your long-range training calendar, how many miles will your unit move in one year?

—Get advice from the battalion executive officer or battalion S-4.

- **Purchase only what you're authorized**—If in doubt, research and ask questions. Never buy first and ask questions later.
- **Have weekly or bi-weekly budget briefings**—Your budget officer should give you a status report. Periodically check his math.
- **Develop a simple tracking system for your expenditures.**
    —Your battalion executive officer or S-4 should already have a system for subordinate units' use.
    —Track your budget by class, dollar amount, and budget quarter.
- **Commit your money as early as possible.**
    —A 30 to 35 percent commitment rate at the end of the first quarter is good.
    —Put your unit in a position to receive last-minute funds from battalion at the end of the fiscal year.
    —Most Divisions or Corps cut off spending by mid-September to allow requisitions in the system to hit at year end. If you have money left on 15 September, you lose it.
- **Don't over obligate**—If your budget is $50,000 for the year, don't spend more than $50,000. It's irresponsible—and illegal.
- **Stay involved.**
    —Supervision prevents waste and abuse of funds.
    —If you're constantly involved in your unit financial matters, you're taking care of your soldiers.

Let's go back to the beginning for a moment . . .

Remember the tent "loan"?
- Do you give the tent to your buddy? If so, how do you justify such an action to your platoon leader?

- Should you talk with your supply sergeant? Your battalion S-4? Your battalion executive officer? Your lawyer?
- Who should you see to correct the unwieldy turn-in procedures?

Answer these questions in light of what you've read in this chapter. If you don't know the answers, you should know where to find them. Do you now see how important your supply responsibilities are?

The Bottom Line
for
Supply

- RESPONSIBILITY. You're the catalyst for accurate property accountability. You're totally responsible for all property in your unit. You can delegate accountability, but not command responsibility.

- PROPERTY ACCOUNTABILITY DECISIONS AREN'T MADE IN A VACUUM. Your battalion S-4, property book officer, executive officer, commander, and lawyer all will help you make smart decisions. Talk with them.

- MONEY TALKS. Lose Army property, damage it, destroy it—you buy it. Be sure your soldiers know this.

- INVENTORIES. The change-of-command, monthly 10–percent, and sensitive-item inventories are *musts* for you to accomplish *personally*.

- PROPERTY RECORDS. Check and recheck them for accuracy and accountability.

- PROPERTY RECORDS ADJUSTMENT. If someone in your unit doesn't pay, you will pay on your departure. If the property is on the books, it better be in the company.

- YOUR BUDGET. Monitor it frequently. It's your unit's money. It buys combat readiness.

Bibliography for Supply

AR 710-2, *Supply Policy Below the Wholesale Level.*

AR 735-5, *Policies and Procedures for Property Accountability.*

DA Pam 25-30, *Consolidated Index to Administrative Publications and Blank Forms.*

DA Pam 710-2-1, *Using Unit Supply System Manual Procedures.*

FM 10-14-3, *Surveying Officer's Guide.*

TC 710-5, *Unit Commander's Supply Handbook.*

Unit Supply Update.

8. Maintenance

Fighting and winning the next war is not always the result of brilliant tactics and masterful strategy— for without well-maintained equipment all the tactics and strategy in the world are for naught.

A Wise Commander

THIS COULD HAPPEN TO YOU—Vehicle safety is a high-priority task in this company. The motor pool prides itself on its strict quality control procedures. The unit's maintenance standing operating procedure (SOP) directs that after a mechanic completes his services, the shop foreman inspects the vehicle and the motor sergeant—using the technical inspection checklist—spot checks deadlining items. This procedure worked well until the motor sergeant went on emergency leave. The shop foreman, who recently arrived in the unit, temporarily assumed the motor sergeant's duties. Specialist Jones, a unit mechanic, did the annual service for Jeep No. 583-6. However, Jones sometimes gets sidetracked and forgets to finish certain tasks. He means well, but he needs close supervision. Besides, his wife just had their second child. Because both children are under two, Jones worries a lot about making ends meet.

Specialist Jones tells the shop foreman he's finished with the annual service on Jeep No. 583-6 and it's ready to be checked. Because the shop foreman is busy completing a report the company commander needs by noon, he only quickly checks the mechanic's work. In addition, the shop foreman, working outside his MOS, isn't as familiar with M151-A2s as he should be. Everything looks okay from the outside, but he fails to check the deadlining items and passes the vehicle.

During the next operational readiness test, as the company commander's driver is steering Jeep No. 583-6 around a corner, the right front wheel falls off. The vehicle overturns. The driver suffers two broken legs and a dislocated shoulder. The accident investigation reveals, among other things, that the mechanic failed his last two SQTs (one taken at his previous unit). The cause of the accident was a missing cotter pin in the front wheel; the pin was removed when the bearings were repacked, but was never replaced.

NOW WHAT HAPPENS, COMPANY COMMANDER? What should have been done to prevent the injury to the driver and damage to the jeep?

The Company Commander's Maintenance Responsibilities

You have two major maintenance responsibilities: *Maintain* your equipment in fully mission-capable status, and *train* your crews, operators, and leaders to maintain equipment.

MAINTAIN: Maintaining *all* your equipment is tough work, but someone *has* to do it. You may command the best-trained infantry, armor, or signal company in the US Army, but if your equipment isn't properly maintained and fully mission-capable, you can't shoot, move, or communicate. Assign responsibility for every piece of equipment in the company. Don't downplay the importance of maintenance— without it, you can't perform, and every aspect of your unit training is in jeopardy.

TRAIN: Training your operators and crews to use and maintain their equipment properly is just as important as training them to do their particular jobs in the Army. Also, train your subordinate leaders to supervise maintenance operations properly. An *effective* preventive maintenance system demands total unit involvement. If a unit commander can motivate his or her soldiers to perform preventive maintenance checks and services properly, he can motivate his soldiers to do everything.

Educate Yourself

REVIEW REGULATIONS AND INSPECTION RE-PORTS: Just as you reviewed property accountability regulations, review maintenance regulations:

- DA Pam 750-1, *Organizational Maintenance Guide For Leaders*.
- DA Pam 750-35, *Functional Users Guide For Motor Pool Operations*.
- DA Pam 738-750, *The Army Maintenance Management System (TAMMS)*.

Don't memorize them; just become familiar with them. DA Pam 750-1 is the most useful document for you as a company commander because it briefly highlights all major maintenance matters the commander must be aware of.

Review the last two or three battalion maintenance reports, the last Inspector General report, and the last Material Assistance and Inspection Team (MAIT) report. Note any recurring deficiencies or trends and use them as a starting point in developing your maintenance program. If your predecessor did her job correctly, most recurring deficiencies will have been corrected. If not, you must direct your motor officer and motor sergeant to correct them.

TALK WITH KEY INDIVIDUALS: Your *battalion motor officer and motor sergeant* are the most knowledgeable sources for "outside" information about your maintenance operation. They wrote the battalion inspection reports you reviewed. Discuss their findings with them. Their job is to support you. Keep them aware of your problems and ask them for help when you need it.

Your *battalion executive officer* usually is the maintenance czar for the battalion. He'll give you the overall maintenance posture of the battalion and his opinion of your maintenance program. If you need a field-grade officer's expertise with a problem, go to him. He can supply battalion-level leverage—if you should need it.

Don't forget your *fellow company commanders*. Ask them what they did to develop and sustain a solid maintenance program:

- What maintenance problems did you encounter when you assumed command?
- Does the battalion maintenance inspection accurately reflect your maintenance posture?
- Does the "old man" have any particular maintenance quirks?
- How helpful and prompt is the direct-support maintenance unit?
- Do you have a solid Preventive Maintenance Checks and Services (PMCS) program? If so, what's your secret?

You're now ready to talk with the *battalion commander*. Listen first, then ask questions on items you're still not clear about. As always, don't leave the office until you know his expectations and maintenance standards.

VISIT KEY ORGANIZATIONS: A visit to your *direct-support unit* (DSU) for maintenance is worth its weight in transmission parts. This unit provides you with maintenance repair, technical assistance, and repair parts. When you visit the DSU, ask for a mission briefing and tour the facility. While touring, check if your unit has any problems you should know about:

- Is your unit picking up completed work orders daily?
- How frequently does the DSU inspection team reject your equipment?
- Does the DSU commander provide contact-team support?
- What maintenance assistance training does he have for your maintenance programs?

A visit to your DSU every month or two will keep you abreast of your maintenance challenges.

Visit your *local MAIT*. As you talk about property accountability, ask about maintenance too.

LEARN FROM THOSE WHO KNOW.

War Story

General John A. Wickham, Jr., Army Chief of Staff, 1985-88, related the following experience: When he graduated from West Point in 1950, he was assigned to a weapons platoon in Europe. The platoon had 57mm recoilless rifles and 60mm mortars, among other weapons. He didn't know a 57 from a 60 or, as he said, "I didn't know my ear from my elbow" about these weapons. However, he had an outstanding platoon sergeant—Sergeant First Class Putnam. In order to make "the lieutenant" knowledgeable about the weapons, SFC Putnam asked Lieutenant Wickham if he'd like to learn the weapons' crew drill. The lieutenant jumped at the opportunity. His unit was training in Grafenwohr, Germany, and, for the next 10 days, after supper, SFC Putnam took Lt. Wickham to a muddy spot next to the latrine for weapons training. At first, Lt. Wickham had no idea why Putnam picked this location for the training, but he soon learned why. After supper, every soldier in the unit usually visited the latrine and inevitably looked over the screen and saw their platoon sergeant teaching the new lieutenant the crew drill. The soldiers instantly knew their lieutenant cared and was willing to learn from their platoon sergeant. Putnam obviously knew what he was doing. Take advantage of anyone, regardless of rank, who can teach you how to do your job better. Don't be too proud or too dumb.

Next week, you'll inspect the second platoon's vehicles. This inspection will be your first vehicle inspection since assuming command. One evening, the week *before* the inspection, ask your motor sergeant to meet you in the motor pool after duty hours.

Tip Make it a hands-on session, by which you can get "maintenance" smart. Ask him to show you the best way to inspect your vehicles and the most common first-echelon deficiencies usually found. Your unit's maintenance posture will improve if you have "hands-on" involvement. This tip applies to any functional area in your company. Don't hesitate to get educated; the result is a combat-ready unit.

Educate Your Unit

SET THE EXAMPLE: Rest assured, unless you take a personal and active interest in your maintenance program, you won't have one. How many soldiers do you know who get "turned on" by maintenance? Maintenance isn't glamorous, but it's critical to your unit's survival on the battlefield. Visit your motor pool daily; observe your platoon leaders and platoon sergeants conducting maintenance training. Make frequent checks of your vehicles, weapons, and other equipment.

Tip On your OER support form, include, as one of your objectives, an effective maintenance program, with emphasis on improved operator performance through training of operators and supervisors. Ensure your lieutenants include maintenance objectives on their support form.

CONDUCT UNIT CLASSES: Hands-on maintenance training should be an integral part of your training program and annotated on your training schedule. Teach **EVERY** soldier in your unit how to perform PMCS on **EVERY** piece of equipment he or she may come in contact with. And don't forget—you and your officers must excel at PMCS, too.

★ ★ ★ ★ ★ *THE BRASS SAYS*

Major General Albin Wheeler on maintenance training: I have never seen a unit that had a super maintenance program unless it put maintenance into the training program and it became an everyday living, breathing, talking part of what soldiers do.

War Story

A company commander had his work cut out for him when he took command of a poor unit. He made dramatic improvements in every aspect of the unit, except his motor pool and vehicle maintenance. After his unit "boloed"—for the second time—the battalion maintenance inspection, and after a tense visit with the battalion commander, the determined company commander called his unit leadership together. They created a unit maintenance certification course. Every soldier in the unit, including the company commander and first sergeant, took unit maintenance classes, followed by written and hands-on tests. If someone failed the test, he or she went through the class again and was retested until certified. This unit never failed another battalion-level or higher maintenance inspection. In fact, every company in the battalion adopted the commander's maintenance certification course.

SCHEDULE A MAIT VISIT: The same procedures for a property accountability MAIT visit discussed in the previous chapter apply for maintenance:

- Schedule a MAIT visit, only with the approval of your battalion headquarters.
- Ensure maximum soldier participation.
- Request hands-on training as much as possible.
- Follow up on MAIT recommendations for your unit.

CONDUCT LOW-DENSITY TRAINING CLASSES: As with Supply, so with Maintenance:

- Low-density MOS soldiers usually are the least-trained soldiers in your unit.
- You must ensure they receive sufficient training time; a half-day per week as a minimum.
- Close down your sections during the training period—no distractions.

Your maintenance program has three major areas: **Maintenance operations, maintenance management**, and **shop operations**. Your most immediate concern when you take command will be maintenance operations.

Maintenance Operations

PREVENTIVE MAINTENANCE CHECKS AND SERVICES (PMCS): A sustained, supervised PMCS program is the bedrock of an effective maintenance program. Involve the total chain of command in PMCS. **PREVENTION** determines maintenance success, because operators *and* supervisors identify mechanical problems *before* they become serious. Key elements of an effective PMCS program are:

- Units must do PMCS.
- Units must supervise PMCS.
- Always use manuals.
- Always correct faults identified in PMCS before dispatch.

Ensure your dispatcher has the authority to refuse to dispatch a vehicle if it hasn't had a proper PMCS. Have your mechanics routinely spot-check the DA Form 2404 and the vehicle.

Some units conduct PMCS by the numbers, or what is commonly referred to as "motor stables": Every soldier checks the same item, at the same time, on every vehicle in the unit. Put these maintenance periods on your unit's training schedule. You must organize and support these efforts . . . even lead them. Be sure you have adequate time and supplies for the job. However, these scheduled maintenance periods don't eliminate the requirement to accomplish PMCS before dispatching a vehicle.

SCHEDULED SERVICES: DA Pam 750-35 says, "Scheduled maintenance services are the cornerstone of the preventive maintenance program. These services permit the mechanic and maintenance sergeant to assure the correct accomplishment of all unit-level maintenance." Make sure your unit actually performs scheduled services; don't accept a **"penciled-in"** DD Form 314. Spot-check mechanics' and operators' work.

Tip Next time you're in the motor pool, take a look at what your mechanics are doing. If you see a mechanic performing a quarterly service, ask him where his manuals are. If he tells you he doesn't need the manual, because he's done this service a million times before, you've discovered trouble. Check the motor pool bookcase. Unless they're new, manuals should be tattered and greasy. If you're not satisfied, head for your motor sergeant, not the mechanic. It's your motor sergeant's responsibility to monitor the work of his soldiers. Rest assured, the motor sergeant will pass on your "friendly" advice to his mechanics.

Don't fall behind in your scheduled services. If you can't complete services on time, work nights and weekends until you catch up. If you're still behind after the overtime, consider assigning a relieved-of-duty soldier or someone performing extra duty from an Article 15 action to your motor sergeant. These soldiers aren't ideal, but, with proper supervision, they can get the job done. Pick and choose carefully.

CANNIBALIZATION AND CONTROLLED EXCHANGE: *Cannibalization* is the authorized removal of parts from materiel authorized for **disposal**. You're not in the cannibalization business. However, your motor sergeant and his mechanics should visit a cannibalization yard regularly. This yard (the "can point") is an excellent source of repair parts.

According to AR 750-1, *controlled exchange* is "the removal of serviceable parts, components, assemblies and subassemblies from **unserviceable economically reparable materiel** for immediate reuse in restoring a like item of materiel to a mission capable condition." Don't consider controlled exchange a "business-as- usual" procedure. Tightly control it. AR 750-1 is very specific on what guidelines you must follow in parts exchange: "Controlled exchange is authorized only when the required parts, components, or assemblies cannot be obtained from the supply system in time to meet operational readiness requirements." To stay out of trouble, follow these guidelines:

- Meet all controlled exchange regulatory requirements (AR 750-1).
- Authorize controlled exchange only on your approval.
- Inform your battalion S-4 section of the exchange.
- Use controlled exchange as a last resort.

War Story

An engineer company was deactivating, turning in its equipment, and giving away all unauthorized excess materiel. The engineer motor sergeant had tried to "pawn off" two very used jeeps on a signal motor sergeant. The signal motor sergeant said, "Not no, but hell no." The vehicles were in such poor condition and missing so many parts, the signal company would have needed months just to get the vehicles ready for turn-in as scrap metal. Don't accept someone's problem at your expense.

ARMY OIL ANALYSIS PROGRAM (AOAP): Support the AOAP program; it's easy to do right! AOAP, like PMCS, stresses **prevention.** The purpose of AOAP is to find the problems before equipment needs a costly repair. DA Pam 750-5, *AOAP Guide for Leaders*, is your primary resource. Follow these four steps to avoid problems with AOAP:

- Appoint a *conscientious* AOAP monitor.
- Ensure prompt and complete submission of samples.
- Act immediately when the DA Form 3254-R comes back from the laboratory.
- Recognize your AOAP monitor for good duty performance.

CALIBRATION: Calibration or maintenance of Test, Measurement, and Diagnostic Equipment (TMDE) is as easy as AOAP:

- Know which items of equipment in your unit require calibration.
- Periodically spot-check these items, to ensure they're calibrated.
- Appoint a TMDE support coordinator to manage this program for you.

Tip The next time you're in the motor pool, ask your motor officer to explain how she knows when equipment needs calibration. If she stutters and shifts her feet, your calibration program may be non-existent. On the other hand, if she says she uses the monthly calibration listing and TB 43-180-1, move on to the next subject. DA Pam 750-1 provides solid advice: "The mechanic's work may be of little value if tools are not calibrated."

INSPECTIONS: Maintenance inspections give you an objective indicator of your unit's maintenance posture. Inspect your platoon's knowledge on maintenance, as you inspect their equipment. Ask questions. Sometimes announce what items will be inspected, and what information and hands-on training you'll require of your soldiers before an inspection. Who cares if they know the inspection requirements and questions in advance? You're giving them a chance to be proficient in the items you stress. Reward those who work hard and give Saturday training to those who don't.

Maintenance Management

PUBLICATIONS: Ho-hum, we're back to publications again. Stay awake, if you want to stay ahead of the pack. DA Pam 750-1 says, "Publications provide the backbone for your maintenance operation."

★ ★ ★ ★ ★ *THE BRASS SAYS*

Lieutenant General George R. Stotser on maintenance publications: Clearly, the latest publication is as vital to good maintenance as the correct tool.

Check your publications account. Are you receiving the correct and necessary publications? Read *PS* magazine; have your mechanics and operators read it, too. *PS* will keep you current and help improve your maintenance program.

Tip As you're checking maintenance manuals to ensure they're being used, check a few of them against DA Pam 25-30 (*Consolidated Index of Army Publications and Blank Forms*). How many of your regulations are rescinded? Check your microfiche reader. If the reader isn't being used, you know your soldiers aren't using their publications.

THE ARMY MAINTENANCE MANAGEMENT SYSTEM (TAMMS): TAMMS translates to forms and records, and there are plenty of them. You can't become the expert on all of them, but be familiar with their purpose and content. In fact, get your motor sergeant to *show you* the key forms and how you should review them. Your key TAMMS reference is DA Pam 738-750. Don't shrug off the maintenance "paperwork war" too lightly.

One of your most useful forms is the DA Form 2406 (*Material Condition Status Report*). This report lists your equipment status, density, serviceability, and availability. (It's not actually a "TAMMS form"; rather, it's a feeder report you'll use to prepare your unit status report—DA Form 2715.) When you review your 2406, question any item deadlined longer than 30 days. Is it a maintenance or support activity's problem, or is it a delay in receiving a part? Ensure you evacuate items requiring support maintenance work within three days. Your maintenance section should order a part within 48 hours for a deadlined piece of equipment. If your maintenance section isn't meeting those time constraints, find out why. Complete all forms accurately. Sometimes your maintenance personnel may be tempted to make the unit look better than it is. Don't. If you're making every feasible attempt to fix deadlined equipment and your battalion headquarters knows about your problems, don't worry about your deadlined rate. Make accuracy count.

Tip Have your maintenance section give you a completed *back-side* 2406 daily. (It isn't that big a chore!) It helps you stay on top of the unit's deadlined equipment. The back-side 2406 tells you the exact status of all your deadlined equipment—when, why, how long, and who's fixing it. You'll need that information.

PRESCRIBED LOAD LIST (PLL): This list tells you what and how many repair parts you may keep on hand. Locate a good PLL clerk. You'll realize his worth when he goes on leave, so cross train your TAMMS clerk.

Unit PLLs have mandatory parts lists (MPLs). MPL items are combat-essential repair parts. Consequently, you don't have as much flexibility with MPLs as you do with PLLs. A few simple checks will assure you maintain combat readiness:

- Check your PLL listing for accuracy.
- Check PLL storage bins to see that the number of items in the bin agrees with the number listed on the DA Form 3318.
- Keep zero-balance percentage below 10 percent and be sure all zero-balance lines are on valid requisitions.

DISPATCH PROCEDURES: Although your dispatcher probably is a young specialist or private first class, he should have your authority to say *no* to anyone, regardless of rank—and everyone should know it. If this young specialist dispatches a vehicle improperly, he may be putting the vehicle operator in danger and your career on the line. Follow these key dispatching steps:

- Perform a before-operation PMCS check of the vehicle.
- Have the operator's supervisor certify the PMCS was completed properly.
- Have a mechanic spot-check the PMCS (DA Form 2404).
- Have the operator correct the faults he can correct and have a mechanic fix the rest.
- Be sure the operator departs with proper forms and follows the during-operation PMCS.
- Be sure the operator, on return, completes the after-operation PMCS and the dispatcher completes the paperwork.
- Support your dispatcher.

LICENSING PROCEDURES: Although it's easy to rubber-stamp licensing procedures, *don't.* An effective licensing program needs effective driver training and a trained qualifying official (such as the motor sergeant or platoon sergeant). Your qualifying official should be school-trained, thorough, and demanding. Have each driver complete a road test that includes day, night, city, and highway driving. You may want to include a written test. Certainly, hands-on PMCS testing should be a part of the test.

While you're at the motor pool checking motor stables, have three or four soldiers give you their Standard Form 46, *Motor Vehicle Operator's Identification Card*. Cross-check data on the license with your unit's DA Form 348, *Operator's Qualification Record*. Data on both documents must agree.

Tip

RECOGNITION: Challenge your motor officer to make the maintenance awards program an ongoing project. Award the **Mechanic Badge** when a mechanic qualifies by demonstrating superior proficiency in equipment operation.

Award the **Driver Badge** when an operator qualifies by driving 8,000 accident-free miles with no traffic violations or 12 consecutive months with no accidents or tickets. Award these badges *publicly*.

If you really want to take care of your mechanics, encourage your battalion commander to develop a mechanic-of-the-quarter program. Everybody likes to be in the spotlight now and then; maintenance troops are no different.

ON-THE-JOB TRAINING (OJT) AND CROSS-TRAINING: You must have more than one person to cover key jobs in the motor pool. If you can't get where you need to go, you can't do your mission. Use both OJT and cross-training to prepare your motor pool for key personnel absences. OJT follows a formal program that eventually leads to a secondary MOS. Cross-training is less formalized, but, if you practice it religiously, it can compensate well for the lack of school-trained personnel. Keep your maintenance program two-deep at every key position. Training extension course (TEC) tapes, correspondence courses, and the MAIT can help your unit with an OJT or cross-training program.

Shop Operations

SHOP LAYOUT: The sole objective of proper shop layout is efficiency. Standardize your layout so that everyone from the mechanic to the soldier-driver can establish a work routine. On your first two or three visits to the motor pool, ask yourself these questions:

- Is the shop layout logical?
- Is the layout conducive to efficient work flow?
- Are tools and other equipment easily accessible to the mechanics?
- Is the shop office strategically located to control flow of people and paperwork?

FM 29-2, *Organizational Maintenance Operations*, is a good reference.

SHOP APPEARANCE: The appearance of your motor pool reflects directly on your unit and *you*. Don't fall into the trap of justifying a dirty, greasy, sloppy motor pool just because that is the "nature" of their business. Make sure motor pool workers clean their areas at the close of business each day.

STANDING OPERATING PROCEDURES (SOP): DA Pam 750-1 outlines the importance of an SOP: "If your SOP is complete, if you and all other unit personnel have a good working knowledge of its provisions and you're satisfied it's being implemented, your maintenance program has a solid foundation!" Consult FM 29-2 and FM 750-35 for sample SOPs, or ask your local MAIT or IG for copies of good maintenance SOPs. Then, make sure your unit follows the SOP.

If you have a little spare time while you're at the motor pool one day, check tool control procedures. Observe how tools are issued, secured, and maintained, and how the accountability process is managed. After you observe the process, ask the lowest-ranking private (mechanic) for a copy of the maintenance SOP. Surely, he **Tip** will know exactly where it is, because he uses it frequently. Thank him for his assistance and then see if tool control procedures are included in the SOP. If so, do written procedures coincide with what you observed? Remember, if the SOP isn't used, it's useless. If your on-the-spot check shows excellent control procedures, make it a point to compliment the responsible soldier. Do it so the mechanics hear you.

TOOL ROOM: Tool accountability is not just a change-of-command item. Inventory tools periodically, using updated component lists and hand receipts. If your unit doesn't already have them, construct shadow boards and layouts to help keep track of shop tools. (The Air Force uses foam mats in which tools are placed—as in a jig-saw puzzle—to prevent their being left in engine intakes.)

Let's go back to the beginning for a moment . . .

Remember, your driver injured in vehicle No. 583-6?
● What could have prevented this injury?

- Should the shop foreman have detected the missing cotter pin during the PMCS of the vehicle?
- How did your quality control procedure in the motor pool fail for vehicle No. 583-6?
- Who should have established and supervised your maintenance cross-training program?
- More basic, do you *have* a maintenance training program for your motor pool personnel?
- Why didn't you know that Jones had failed his last two skill qualification tests?
- What disciplinary or punitive action will you take against your shop foreman and Jones?
- How will you replace the injured driver while he's recovering?

Answer these questions in light of what you've read in this chapter. If you don't know the answers, you should know where to find them. Do you now see how important your maintenance responsibilities are?

The Bottom Line
for
Maintenance

- YOUR MAINTENANCE RESPONSIBILITIES. Train your soldiers to maintain the unit's equipment properly.

- PMCS. This is the foundation of your maintenance program.

- SCHEDULED SERVICES. Don't "pencil in" and don't fall behind.

- CONTROLLED EXCHANGE. Your approval of controlled exchange is a must.

- TAMMS/PLL/MPL. Get a soldier who *knows* what to do.

- DISPATCHER. Give your dispatcher the authority to say NO.

- RECOGNITION. Award good motor pool performance.

- SHOP OPERATION AND APPEARANCE. Be sure they reflect well on you and your unit.

Bibliography for Maintenance

DA Pam 738-750, *The Army Maintenance Management System (TAAMS)*.

DA Pam 750-1, *Organizational Maintenance, Guide for Leaders*.

DA Pam 750-5, *Army Oil Analysis Program, Guide for Leaders*.

DA Pam 750-35, *Functional Users Guide for Motor Pool Operations*.

FM 29-2, *Organizational Maintenance Operations*.

9. Other Important Command Matters

A commander must try to be all things to all soldiers at all times.

Old Army Saying

THE OLD KITCHEN SINK: By now, you may feel you've been hit with everything but the kitchen sink . . . well, not quite yet. Other important command responsibilities need your attention, and here they are (not in any particular order of importance):

- INTEGRITY.
- INSPECTIONS: A WORD OF ADVICE.
- SAFETY. SAFETY. SAFETY.
- PHYSICAL TRAINING.
- UNIT SPORTS.
- DRUG ABUSE.
- ALCOHOL ABUSE.
- WEIGHT CONTROL.
- THE CHAPLAIN'S ROLE WITH YOUR COMPANY.
- WORKING WITH THE INSPECTOR GENERAL.
- YOUR SOLDIERS AND THEIR FAMILIES.
- THE UNIT STATUS REPORT.
- AMMUNITION ACCOUNTABILITY.
- SECURITY AWARENESS.

INTEGRITY

More has been written recently about integrity, ethics, and values within the military than perhaps any other subject. No surprise: Integrity underlies everything *we* do in the

Army. A "little bit" of integrity won't suffice. It's the basis of everything you do as a human being, an officer, and a commander. It builds trust and confidence between you and your soldiers. A lapse in integrity is catastrophic for you and your company: One slip, one breach—and your soldiers lose trust in what they train daily to do.

Dishonesty is not confined to rank. The following examples demonstrate how integrity affects every rank and every unit:

• A noncommissioned officer goes to Rhein Main Air Force Base, West Germany, to catch a military "hop" to the States. He knows the rules: He must be on leave before he can place his name on the waiting list. To sign in and place his name on the list, he turns in a leave form that appears authentic but has not been turned in to his unit's leave clerk. After signing up, he returns to his unit, works four days, *then* properly signs out on leave and returns to Rhein Main. Lo and behold, his name has risen to the top of the waiting list and he catches the next plane leaving for the States. Because he didn't sign out of his unit until he actually departed for the states, he saved (stole) four days of leave. He also pushed himself ahead of others waiting properly for a hop. If this NCO sees no wrong in doing this, where else will he compromise his integrity?

• A maintenance officer continually asks his mechanics to work on his privately owned vehicle (POV) in the motor pool during duty hours. The mechanics use government tools, equipment, and time. The mechanics now are also working on their own POVs because of the maintenance officer's example. If this officer sees no wrong in this practice, in what other circumstances will he compromise his integrity?

• A personnel specialist intentionally adds five undeserved points to the promotion records of her boyfriend, helping him meet the promotion cut-off score. If this personnel specialist sees no wrong in doing this, what might she do to her squad leader's records after she receives an adverse counseling statement?

You must convince your soldiers that a breach of integrity is never condoned, encouraged, or rewarded. You set both a personal and a professional example: *Demand* that your troops follow. For practical purposes, two good references for unit classes on integrity and ethics are the case studies in TC 22-9-1, *Military Professionalism (Platoon/ Squad Instruction)*, and TC 22-9-2, *Military Professionalism (Company/Battery Instruction)*.

INSPECTIONS; A WORD OF ADVICE

The Army's inspection policies evolve with time. A few years ago, inspections were totally compliance-oriented. But some authorities believed that the Army was going in the wrong direction when units began to "paint the grass green and the rocks white" to get ready for the Inspector General. Today, the Army's emphasis has shifted from IG *compliance* inspections to IG *systemic* inspections, plus inspections by battalion-level and higher headquarters called *command* inspections. With this new emphasis on command scrutiny, inspections are now primarily command responsibilities.

★ ★ ★ ★ ★ *THE BRASS SAYS*

General William J. Livsey, Jr., on inspections: Once upon a time there was Saturday morning. On Saturday morning somebody at some command level—company, battalion, or General Officer—inspected the unit. It was a time for the unit to look at itself. Then somebody said we are only going to work five days a week. Some guys in the Army did not have sense enough to put Saturday morning somewhere else in the week. They turned over the responsibility to look at themselves to the IG, or some Technical Inspection Team, or the MAIT. I think it is downright criminal to call an ordnance technical team to inspect machine guns. Why, for heavens sakes! You mean we don't have sergeants who understand how to assemble and disassemble a machine gun and can tell if something is worn or a part is needed? That's really ridiculous. Inspections are a command responsibility.

As the commander, you are now both the inspect**or** and the inspect**ee**. You are responsible for your unit seven days a week; don't pass the buck up the chain unless you have to.

When You're the Inspector:

• CONDUCT ANNOUNCED INSPECTIONS. Let everyone concerned know in advance **WHEN** you'll inspect and **WHAT** you'll inspect. Publish your inspection agenda in time for your first sergeant, platoon leaders, and platoon sergeants to conduct their own preliminary inspection. Then stick to your schedule. Don't play hurry-up-and-wait with your NCOs. If you show up two hours late and then saunter through an announced inspection—after your soldiers have worked hard to get ready—you lower unit morale. In some ways, such a delay is worse for your soldiers than if you show up on schedule and chew them out for things you find wrong. If you must cancel an inspection, do so as *early* as possible and let your troops know why you've changed plans.

Have your subordinate leaders conduct an inspection *BEFORE* your inspection. Then you place the responsibility for the inspection where it belongs, with your subordinate leaders. If a platoon leader then comes to you the day before an inspection and says he needs a two-day extension because he and the platoon **Tip** sergeant aren't satisfied with their results, give him at least an extra day. Of course, you want to make such extensions the exception, not the rule. Also, encourage your leaders to stay for "GI parties." They don't have to do the manual labor, but they should provide guidance on standards. Soldiers respect a leader who cares about their doing well on inspections.

• CONDUCT UNANNOUNCED INSPECTIONS. If you really want to get an accurate picture of the day-to-day activities of your unit, conduct an unannounced inspection. Unannounced inspections separate the professional soldiers from the rest. Think of unannounced inspections as pop quizzes. Remember the sinking feeling in your stomach when a teacher popped an unannounced quiz on you? Well, your platoon leader, armorer, and motor sergeant may have the same feeling when you conduct an unannounced inspection and they aren't ready. Be assured, though, they'll be prepared the next time. Unannounced inspections keep your soldiers ready for anything at anytime. And when a pop inspection goes very well . . . it's great for company morale.

War Story

One day, while walking past one of his units, a brigadier general observed a young soldier crawling in a window on the first floor of the billets. Thinking that maneuver was a little strange, the general decided to visit the unit. The company commander was in the middle of a training meeting when the general walked in—unannounced. "Hello, captain, how are you today?" asked the general. The captain was dumbfounded, as was everyone else in the room. All he could think to say was, "How may I help you, sir?" The general said he just wanted to stop by and look around the unit because he'd just seen a young troop crawling in a billet window. By the time the general had "looked around," the commander, and most of his soldiers, were ready to climb out a billet window. The unit wasn't prepared for anyone's unannounced visit, much less a BG's. The general gave the captain and his battalion commander 30 days to prepare the unit for his return visit. One hates to imagine what life in that unit was like for 30 days, but, when the general did his follow-up, he was pleasantly surprised by what he found. He also took the time to explain to the young commander the lesson to be learned: ALWAYS BE PREPARED. (Incidentally, the young soldier knocked his shoe onto the ground from where it had been drying on a window ledge. Too lazy to go out the door, he simply crawled out the window . . . and you know the rest.) Murphy's law strikes again.

• DEVELOP THE RIGHT MIX. You need to have a balanced unit inspection program, which mixes announced and unannounced inspections. Inspect sections and the whole unit. Inspect billets and operational areas. The mix and timing are up to you and your first sergeant. But keep inspections to the minimum. You want to minimize disruption to your training and maintenance programs.

• CONDUCT USEFUL INSPECTIONS. Inspections should always have a teaching value. Don't inspect just to have something to do on Friday afternoon. Have a definite purpose: To see if last month's IG deficiencies are fixed; to prepare for the battalion inspection next week, and so forth. In fact, "leaking" what's on your mind before you inspect doesn't hurt. Then you know at least *those items* will be fixed.

Make sure you and your leaders see what you are inspecting. After a while, inspections, like anything else, become routine and you simply go through the motions. A good inspector is always alert, knowledgeable, and attentive to detail. Develop a pattern for **Tip** inspecting a room, for example. Look up (top of wall lockers); look to your left, right, front, rear, and to the floor; then look inside lockers, drawers, and refrigerators. Once you establish a *complete* pattern—don't vary. Teach your platoon leaders this orderly inspection skill. If you're inexperienced in this area, observe your 1SG or watch your battalion CSM inspect a room. They probably mastered the art years ago.

When you inspect, make sure the soldier knows you were there. For example, when you inspect unit TA-50 equipment, as you pick **Tip** up a canteen to inspect it, don't put it back exactly in the same location. Put it to one side, so the soldier knows you were there. However, avoid extremes, like tossing the equipment everywhere. That's like sarcasm—both alienate, not instruct.

• USE A CHECKLIST. Give the checklist to everyone to be inspected *in advance*. What do you care if they know what you'll be looking for? Your goal is to ensure your soldiers are ready and their equipment is in order. Use the same checklist your battalion or brigade headquarters uses. Their purpose, like yours, is to keep your unit combat ready. You're better off if you both check the same readiness items.

- EMPHASIZE THE GOOD AS WELL AS THE BAD. It's easy to find things wrong, but avoid the tendency to focus only on the inspection's negative findings. Make sure you acknowledge the positive points also—by leaving a note or praising publicly. A lot of preparation went into that inspection. Acknowledge your soldiers' hard work, and encourage them to do even better next time.

- FOLLOW UP. Make sure the deficiencies you find are corrected or your inspection is a wasted effort. *Schedule* a follow-up inspection to check those items that particularly concern you. Give your unit sufficient time to correct deficiencies before the follow-up. You don't want a sloppy, haphazard fix. Have the NCO involved make a note of what you want fixed. Ask to see that note next time you inspect. You'll help *him* and yourself.

War Story

A hard-charging, experienced company commander developed an "Area–a–Day" inspection program. He spent 30 to 60 minutes every day inspecting something. He scheduled these short inspections in advance. He did inspections on the first three days of the week and used Thursday and Friday for follow-up inspections on deficiencies of the previous week's inspections. At first, the unit screamed, "Overkill!" But, after a while, the unit saw the results of the company commander's persistence: Sustained high standards.

Better yet, the commander occasionally delegated the daily inspection to a platoon leader. This procedure quickly opened the lieutenant's eyes, especially since the shoe was on the other foot. Thursday and Friday were key

> *days in his inspection program. Follow-up inspections were as important as the inspection itself. Eventually, the number of Thursday and Friday inspections gradually fell off and the unit knew it had met or exceeded the commander's high standards.*

When You're the Inspectee:

• BE PREPARED. Don't take any announced inspection lightly. *Always* present your unit in the best light possible. In fact, establish a unit mind-set to treat all inspections alike: Best boot forward.

War Story

A new battalion commander published his command inspection program and schedule for each company. Company A was to be inspected Tuesday at 0900 hours. The company headquarters was located on the third floor of its building. When the battalion commander drove up at 0900 hours—no one was at the curb to escort him. He made his own way into the building and up to the company commander's office. When the commander said, "Oh, Sir, we've been expecting you," disaster struck: "Why wasn't someone out there to meet me? You knew I was coming, didn't you?" The word quickly spread throughout the battalion and there were no more repeat performances. The captain quickly learned something about military courtesy (and good judgment) he'd never find in a manual.

• DON'T "CRAM" FOR AN INSPECTION. Your goal is to develop a **sustained** inspection program in your unit. Maintain your standards *daily*, not just prior to a major inspection. BUT, BE REASONABLE, NOT "HYPER." Some peaking takes place for an inspection, but soldiers get frustrated if they constantly peak for inspections. Soldiers will sustain high standards if they're reasonable, consistent, and enforced.

• DON'T FORGET YOUR FREE COMMAND INSPECTION. Remember these lines from AR 1-201, *Inspections*? "All newly assigned commanders and detachment commanders will receive a free command inspection from their immediate supervisor within 90 days of assuming command." Don't pass up this "freebie." Consult your first sergeant about *when* to ask for this inspection.

• REQUEST ASSISTANCE VISITS. It's better to find and fix a problem during a battalion or brigade assistance visit than have it discovered during a command inspection. Requesting assistance visits isn't a sign of weakness; it's a sign of wisdom.

SAFETY. SAFETY. SAFETY

How important *is* safety? Here are some facts collected by the staff of *Officer's Call*:

FACT: In World War II, **one out of every five** American soldiers killed, died because of an accident.

FACT: In Korea, **more than half** of all Army personnel hospitalized suffered their injuries due to accidents.

FACT: In Vietnam, **nearly five million** nondisabling injuries resulted from accidents—and more than 5,700 lives were lost in accidents.

FACT: Today, the equivalent of a **battalion** of soldiers is killed each year in accidents.

FACT: Today, the Army loses the equivalent of an **entire mechanized infantry brigade** for more than six weeks each year because of injuries from accidents.

FACT: If the money that accidents cost could be spent on weapons, **150 new M1 Abram tanks** could be placed in the field each year.

FACT: If the money spent each year on accidents were saved and spent on aviation assets, **150 new attack helicopters** could be put into service **annually.**

If these facts don't get your attention about safety, check the safety record of the unit you are about to command. Where does it stand?

Training is your most important **mission**, but safety is your most important **task**. Safety is paramount in the field, the motor pool, the dining facility, the arms room, the billet rooms—EVERYWHERE AND ALL THE TIME. Your safety program must be real and geared to your training mission.

★ ★ ★ ★ ★ *THE BRASS SAYS*

General John A. Wickham's five-point philosophy on safety:
1. Nothing we do in peacetime warrants the unnecessary risk of life or equipment.
2. Commanders are safety officers.
3. Instill in soldiers a sixth sense of safety.
4. Fix accountability.
5. Be proactive and aggressive.

General John A. Wickham's five-point safety philosophy is on a video tape and is available for distribution to Army units. Review this tape. Show it to every soldier in your unit and make it a part of your orientation briefing for all new soldiers arriving in your unit.

Tip

Incorporate the following important elements into your own safety program:

● STRESS safety as a way of life. Your safety program must be vibrant; it can't be a paper drill. Your soldiers must treat safety as if their lives depended on it, because they do.

(Approximately 80 percent of all Army accidents involve human error.)

• DON'T delegate your safety responsibilities. Appoint (on orders) yourself as the unit safety officer and your first sergeant as the unit safety NCO. True, you and your 1SG will have others helping you, but you and your 1SG will be—must be—deeply involved in *your* unit's safety program.

• TAKE acceptable risks. Live-fire exercises are necessary training events for soldiers. They can't be excluded by the fear that a soldier may get hurt. Take every possible safety precaution, but conduct the live-fire exercise.

• HAVE an active unit safety council. DA Pam 385-1, *Unit Safety Management*, explains the formation and function of a unit safety council. (This pamphlet also will help you formulate your entire unit safety program.) You run the safety council, you attend all meetings, and you make it happen.

• MAKE safety awards a reality. It's easy to find the safety problems in a unit, but much harder to find positive safety recognition. Make your soldiers safety-conscious by awarding their peers who point out safety problems and make corrections.

• ANALYZE your accidents. Too many times, a commander gets "wrapped around the axle" over the accident itself, rather than analyzing possible causes for it. Study your accident reports. You may discover a trend you can reverse.

War Story

*One frustrated battalion commander started a "Come–See–***The–Man***"* time because the military vehicle accident rate in his battalion was off the chart. His battalion had more military vehicle accidents than any other unit in the division—a distinction he loathed.

If a soldier had an at-fault military vehicle accident, the soldier and his entire chain of command had to visit the battalion commander and the CSM to explain the who, what, where, when, how, and why of the accident.

They had to use charts and viewgraphs that helped depict the accident. Then the battalion commander and the CSM asked pointed *questions: Was the vehicle properly dispatched? Did the squad leader supervise and certify a proper PMCS program? What were this soldier and his unit now doing to prevent future accidents?*

The battalion commander and CSM's questions forced the soldier and his unit leaders to put the accident under a microscope. As a result, the at-fault military vehicle accident rate decreased dramatically.

• GIVE safety briefings. How many times have you ignored the pre-holiday POV safety briefing or done it haphazardly? How many times have you paid mere lip service to your hot- and cold-weather safety classes, or drown-proofing class, or hearing injury protection briefing? Preaching safety is as important as practicing it.

• HAVE a safety SOP. Your safety SOP **must** be current and useful.

PHYSICAL TRAINING (PT)

If you don't do physical training, why should anyone else? Leading by example in PT doesn't mean you have to run faster or do more push-ups and sit-ups than any other soldier in your unit. However, it does mean you have to give your best effort and demand the same from everyone else.

PT has two purposes: To develop physical stamina required for combat, and to develop unit esprit-de-corps. Soldiers must be physically prepared at all times. Wars usually are come-as-you-are. You won't have time to get in shape; you have to *stay* in shape, through PT. And unit PT has the added benefit of building morale and boosting unit cohesion.

★ ★ ★ ★ ★ *THE BRASS SAYS*

John O. Marsh, Jr., Secretary of the Army, on physical training: The readiness of the United States Army begins with the physical fitness of the individual soldier and the non-commissioned officers and officers who lead them.

War Story

One company commander took command of his unit and quickly realized the unit's PT program had no substance. He organized a program of daily PT that would get everyone in shape. Shortly after the third PT session, many soldiers complained that the three-mile run was too fast, while others complained it was too slow. The captain had set a standard for the three-mile run at eight-and-a-half minutes per mile.

Some soldiers wanted to divide the unit into two sections for the run—fast and slow groups. The new commander was adamant that the unit should stay together. He told the soldiers who wanted to form a slow group that his PT standard for the run was eight-and-a-half minutes per mile, and that they should work toward that standard. He told the soldiers who wanted to form a fast group that they could run further and faster after they completed the unit run. He knew that unit morale and esprit-de-corps would suffer if he allowed the unit to divide, even in PT.

The commander also knew that to develop the aerobic capacity in the faster soldiers, he had to let them run faster and further. However, he felt strongly that the esprit-de-corps benefit of a unit run outweighed the aerobic benefit. He developed aerobic capacity with other exercises.

193

Make sure your unit PT program has these characteristics:

• MANDATORY: Allow no exceptions for unit PT. A platoon sergeant who's too busy for PT doesn't have a good excuse. Every soldier in the unit, including cooks, mechanics, and clerks, must do PT. You and your first sergeant lead the way—always.

Tip

If you want a quick check of your unit's PT program, check your cooks' program. Do PT with your cooks (unannounced). If their fitness is poor or they pass out at the sight of you doing PT with them, your PT program needs some work.

• ORGANIZED: Plan your PT program the same way you plan your training program. The days of everyone grabbing a basketball and "shooting hoops" for 45 minutes are over. Soldiers should know how far they will have to run before their first step. An organized PT program is a *safe* PT program. Your objective is to condition a soldier, not kill him. Ensure all soldiers receive their periodic physical examinations. Soldiers on profile don't participate.

Out-of-shape soldiers are susceptible to injuries and heart attacks. Establish a gradual program that enables them to meet your standards. Therefore, when you plan your unit PT program, don't

Tip

forget remedial PT. It's a must. Put an NCO or officer in charge of remedial PT who'll keep the pressure on but without unreasonable demands. Make it someone who's willing to encourage and support out-of-shape soldiers until they meet PT standards. Do remedial PT after duty hours.

• INTERESTING: The days of doing the "daily dozen" exercises and running a mile are over. Is anything more boring? You have absolutely no excuse for a boring PT program with all the varied activities you can choose from: Swimming, aerobics, grass drills, guerrilla exercises, obstacle courses, circuits, rifle drill, and competitive fitness events. Take your pick; talk with your soldiers and find out what they want to do for PT. Keep it varied.

War Story

One Armor battalion commander periodically would have one of his company commanders choose a platoon to participate in the "Battalion Commander's PT Tank Drill." The tank platoon would arrive in PT gear. The company commander would give the platoon leader an OPORD to conduct a three- to four-mile dismounted tactical road march. The lieutenant had 20 minutes to prepare his order, brief his platoon, and reach the starting point. Tank crews ran in the same formation they used when seated in a tank. If a member of a crew would fall out or slow down, the entire crew would fall out or slow down. The platoon leader had to decide when to continue, or when to slow the platoon.

This exercise combined demanding physical training with a mission-essential simulation. The PT program was interesting and organized around what soldiers actually did.

- DEMANDING: A soldier should be *tired* but not *exhausted* when he finishes a unit PT session. And he should finish feeling that *his unit* has accomplished something.

Tip If you don't have a soldier in your unit who's a certified Master Fitness Trainer (MFT), get one. He will train your leaders how to conduct PT properly. If necessary, seek an MFT school allocation and send one of your interested, outstanding soldiers to become a certified MFT.

War Story

One demanding company commander was a marathon runner in college. As a result of his interest and ability in running, he forced a very aggressive PT running program on his unit. He frequently led the unit on a six-mile run at a very fast pace, leaving soldiers scattered all over the area. This program boosted the commander's *ego, but it destroyed his soldiers' self-confidence. The pace and distance were unreasonable for the unit as a whole. Only a few avid runners could keep the pace. Consequently, the unit had its "heroes" and "goats." Morale hit rock bottom. Making unrealistic PT demands is bad leadership and can lead to injuries.*

• CHALLENGING: You, your MFT, and your leaders should develop a PT program that is progressively challenging. Once you've established a balanced program, determine how to challenge your soldiers to achieve greater levels of fitness. PT does not always have to be conducted by an NCO who is 6-foot-4, 180 pounds and who could double for the latest Army recruiting poster. Let young, eager PFCs or Specialists lead PT. They're capable, provided their leaders *ensure* they are ready and won't embarrass themselves. What a great confidence builder. Your lieutenants are capable of leading PT. Share the wealth—challenge everyone. If you know your unit is fit for special challenges and you can tie these challenges to training—do it.

War Story

One infantry company commander would incorporate physically challenging missions into routine three-day field exercises. If the company were training in how to capture an enemy position, it would do it via a 10-mile forced road march with full gear. The unit never marched down a road—always cross country at a fast pace. The compass course was always completed in full gear and each squad or platoon was timed between stations. Double time was the minimum acceptable pace. In fact, this company commander combined PT with mission training every chance he got. He knew his soldiers thrived on a challenge and he provided it. They increased their physical stamina, and, at the same time, sharpened their tactical skills and increased their morale.

• FUN: If your PT program is **balanced** (interesting, varied, demanding, and challenging), your soldiers will have some fun. You will, too.

UNIT SPORTS

A unit sports program isn't a substitute for your PT program, but it's a great supplement to it.

★ ★ ★ ★ ★ *THE BRASS SAYS*

Major General Eugene Cromartie on unit sports: A good unit sports program is one of the best tools a commander has to enhance morale and cohesion.

DEVELOP A DIVERSE SPORTS PROGRAM: A good unit sports program involves as many unit soldiers as possible in as many different team sports as possible. Your goal is to develop teamwork and good morale that carry over to your unit's military mission.

War Story

A new company commander took command of a unit that was at the bottom of the battalion heap. The unit had failed its last two command inspections, morale was low, and the previous commander had been unceremoniously relieved of duty. The commander decided that one of her first actions would be to return pride to the unit. As part of her plan, she organized a unit softball team, because she was a good softball player and had spotted several other good players in pickup games. The unit rallied

> *around the team and unit attendance at games tripled by mid-season. At season's end, the team was playing to a standing-room-only crowd. As the team won more games, soldiers started believing in themselves. This belief carried over to the unit's performance on the job. The company developed higher billet standards, achieved better training and maintenance records, and got higher marks on command inspections. The soldiers even asked for unit basketball and volleyball teams. This commander didn't take long to turn her unit around, a process that began with a good unit sports program.*

SUPPORT YOUR PROGRAM: You may be the company commander, but that doesn't automatically make you a jock. You can support a unit sports program in other ways than by participating as a member of every unit team. Your mere presence at unit games is supportive. Attendance increases when the word gets out that the "old man" shows up for the unit's games. Bring your family, too.

DON'T OVERDO IT: Don't push unit sports so much that you lose sight of your Army mission. Don't exempt a soldier from duty so he can take part on a unit sports team; you'll create more morale problems than you fix. A bonafide soldier athlete will do his job and still have time to participate on a unit sports team.

DRUG ABUSE

Eliminating illegal drugs and drug users in your unit is everyone's business. *Every soldier* in your unit must take part in getting rid of illegal drugs and drug users in the Army. Ensure that everyone in your unit is aware of your policy and enforce that policy to the limit of the law. From the list below, pick the answer that best indicates what you want your company's soldiers to think about your philosophy on illegal drugs:

A. Absolute zero tolerance.
B. Professional soldiers don't possess, use, or distribute illegal drugs. Those who do, don't belong in the military.
C. Possession, use, and distribution of illegal drugs is criminal and demonstrates a lack of trustworthiness.
D. Soldiers who possess, use, or distribute drugs damage the reputation and jeopardize the mission of the unit and the Army.

The answer of course, is "all of the above."

Consider the following points when establishing your policy on drugs:

CONSULT YOUR LAWYER: Ensure you thoroughly understand the proper legal action to take when conducting a search and seizure, protecting a soldier's rights, or handling evidence. You can't prosecute drug abusers if your evidence won't stand up in court because it has been seized illegally.

USE URINALYSIS TESTING: Urinalysis tests, which are nothing more than unannounced inspections, are among the best deterrents the Army has to eliminate illegal drug use. Use them frequently and when the troops least expect them. After a holiday weekend is a particularly good time.

Tip When you schedule a unit-wide urinalysis test, be the first person in line to be tested. Your first sergeant should be second in line, followed by the rest of your unit leaders. You're clean and not afraid to show it. And because you're clean, everyone else damn well better be clean, too!

War Story

In 1986, Lieutenant General Andrew P. Chambers, Commander, VII Corps, established Operation Clean Team. *Any VII Corps soldier taking part in a VII Corps-sponsored athletic competition had to pass a urinalysis test before participation.* Operation Clean Team *later was expanded to include squads, platoons, and companies taking part in training events (such as* Grafenwohr Train- ing Center *for a month or any other major field exercise).* Clean Team *stressed teamwork. Every soldier in a unit or on a team had to be clean. Peer pressure mounted—if you're not clean, you're not only harming yourself, but also the entire team, or squad, or platoon. This concept got soldiers' attention and was successful throughout the command.*

USE ANY OTHER LEGAL AND APPROPRIATE MEANS AVAILABLE TO COMBAT UNIT DRUG PROB- LEM: When you conduct a health and welfare inspection, coordinate with the military police so you can use their drug dogs. Coordinate well in advance because the dogs are in demand. If you suspect a drug problem in your unit, talk with the local Criminal Investigation Command (CID) com- mander for suggestions. Use your chaplain or local counse- lors to assist you with drug problems.

War Story

A battalion commander was conducting a "rap session," allowing his soldiers to tell him what they liked and didn't like about the unit. One soldier said he'd just re- ceived a positive urinalysis test result and was relieved of duty pending an investigation. He was adamant about his innocence, and other soldiers were adamantly sup- porting his position. The battalion commander said he would look into the matter and get back to the soldier.

The company commander told the battalion com- mander that he checked the chain of custody and all uri- nalysis paperwork and that everything was in order. The battalion commander, after consulting with a lawyer and the CID, suggested that the company commander arrange a polygraph test for this soldier. The company com- mander liked the idea and the soldier agreed, saying he would do anything to prove his innocence. The word spread throughout the unit. Lo and behold, the soldier flunked the polygraph—big time. The soldier then confessed and admitted his use of drugs.

The battalion commander reconvened the "rap session" with the soldier present and publicly reviewed the entire situation. This time, there was no hue and cry over the soldier's innocence—only dead silence.

TALK WITH YOUR SOLDIERS: If you have a drug problem in your unit, your soldiers know it, and know who the culprits are. You won't get soldiers to talk, however, if you sit in your office all day. Visit the unit at night and on weekends and talk with your soldiers about drug problems in the unit and ask their suggestions on how to eliminate the problems.

ALCOHOL ABUSE

The days of four- and five-hour happy hours are over. Alcohol abuse is usually a greater problem for company commanders than drug abuse. Be very sensitive to how alcohol is used in your unit. Let your soldiers know, early, your position concerning alcohol abuse. Your program on alcohol abuse should consist of four key elements:

PREVENTION: Publish your alcohol abuse policy and let your soldiers know you won't tolerate abuse of alcohol in your unit. Send a signal that alcohol abuse can be "deadly," in more ways than one. If your unit leaders drink, make sure they set the example for responsible drinking. Whatever you do, don't let your chain of command glamorize alcohol. Getting "smashed" or "bombed" is no longer a Friday end-of-the-week way of doing things. Responsible "soldiering" of drinking habits is. Make sure your policy reflects this responsibility.

Tip Anytime you have a unit function where alcohol is present, also have non-alcoholic beverages readily available. Give your soldiers and their families a choice. Support a designated-driver program at *all* unit gatherings.

EDUCATION: You and your unit leaders must know about the Army Drug and Alcohol Prevention and Control Program (ADAPCP). Your soldiers must learn the detrimental effect alcohol abuse has on them and the unit.

Review AR 600-85, *Alcohol and Drug Abuse Prevention and Control Program*. It puts the entire alcohol and drug abuse program in perspective and explains where to get help. Contact your local alcohol and drug control officer and have her or him speak at one of your NCOPD or OPD sessions.

IDENTIFICATION: Identify the soldier with an alcohol problem so you can help that person. Make sure your soldiers know that's your goal. Getting a person with a drinking problem to admit the problem is one of the hardest steps in treating him or her. Most alcoholics deny their problem—vehemently. Families, friends, and coworkers can help you identify your soldiers with alcohol problems.

Tip Occasionally visit the billets late on a weekend evening. Casually walk from room to room observing the parties. Your visit can help you identify the use of alcohol in your unit. More importantly, you might identify some soldier you and your sergeants need to talk to.

REHABILITATION AND TREATMENT: If you consider that even though your soldier has an alcohol problem he is worth saving, be relentless in your pursuit of treatment and rehabilitation. Work closely with the ADAPCP counselor to determine proper treatment. Alcohol rehabilitation is a unit, as well as a command responsibility.

Treatment for alcohol abuse can range from Track I (awareness education and group counseling) to Track III (six to eight weeks of residential medical treatment with nonresidential follow-up). A rehabilitation team consisting of your soldier, you, and the ADAPCP counselor will determine the track for the soldier. Other people may be involved in the treatment—such as spouses, immediate supervisors, community support groups, and the chaplain. These people can recommend courses of action, but *you* make the decisions. Because you'll frequently interact with community support groups, develop good relations with them.

Tip Always attend your soldier's graduation from Track III at the residential treatment facility. It is a very emotional ceremony and merits your support and the support of your first sergeant. In fact, even if you don't have a soldier graduating from Track III, attend a graduation ceremony to get a firsthand idea of what alcohol problems are really all about.

War Story

Alpha company just passed its biggest command inspection. In fact, the company rating was the highest in the brigade. The unit commander invited his senior NCOs and officers to his house that evening for a barbecue to celebrate the superior rating. In the process, some forgot to designate a non-drinking driver. More than one officer and NCO drove away drunk. One of the senior NCOs, a 19-year veteran with two tours in Vietnam, lost control of his car and hit a telephone pole. The investigation revealed he was well above the legal limit for alcohol. He left behind a wife and two boys . . . and a platoon of soldiers.

WEIGHT CONTROL

The Army's weight-control program strives to meet two goals: To make sure all soldiers meet the physical-demands of their job in combat, and to ensure all soldiers present a proper military appearance.

Tip **Just as you and your first sergeant were first in line for the unannounced urinalysis test, be first in line for the unit weigh-in. You lead, and your unit follows.**

FOLLOW THE REGULATIONS: You and your soldiers must be weighed when you take the Army Physical Fitness Test (APFT), or every six months. The mechanics of proper weigh-in procedures, weight tables, composition of body fat, and all other elements of the program are in AR 600-9, *The Army Weight Control Program*. If a soldier is overweight, he receives no favorable personnel actions, including school assignments, promotion, or the privilege of reenlisting. Document the problems and follow up on them for a successful weight-control program.

DON'T MAKE EXCEPTIONS: If you are making exceptions to your weight-control program, you destroy the entire program's credibility with your unit. Be consistent. Let your soldiers know early you'll take whatever action is necessary to enforce Army standards:

- Letters of concern or reprimand.
- Suspension of favorable personnel actions ("flagging").
- Relief of duty.
- Bar to reenlistment.
- Administrative separation.

HELP YOUR OVERWEIGHT SOLDIER: If you insist on a firm weight-control program, you could save a soldier's life, especially if he has a serious overweight problem. Stress the health implications of being overweight and the need for gradual, moderate weight loss. Send overweight soldiers to nutrition classes conducted by qualified health care professionals. Provide additional exercise sessions and food counseling for soldiers who are sincerely trying to lose weight. Compliment your troops when you see they're making progress.

War Story

A company commander had a platoon sergeant who was doing an absolutely outstanding job. However, the platoon sergeant had a weight problem. He had been on and off the weight-control program, had visited the doctor, and was counseled numerous times. The commander had no one to replace the platoon sergeant if he removed him; so he failed to enforce the weight-control program just this once. Other soldiers began to grumble about the double standard for weight control in the unit; it applied to every soldier but the platoon sergeant.

*When the battalion commander heard about the double standard, he acted quickly: "Captain, either you handle this problem according to regulations, or you're history." The company commander promptly flagged the platoon sergeant's records and barred him from reenlistment. The captain also explained the seriousness of the weight problem to the platoon sergeant and his **wife**. Result? The platoon sergeant lost 29 pounds in three months. All he needed to know was that someone was serious about his weight problem.*

THE CHAPLAIN'S ROLE WITH YOUR COMPANY

Your organization and mission will affect how the chaplain functions with your company.

A good chaplain will be:

- **Dedicated** to his faith but tolerant of the views of others.
- **Service-oriented.** His job is to care for you, your soldiers, and your families . . . 24 hours a day.
- **An example.** He'll be a quality soldier and officer. He'll be physically fit and his military appearance will match yours.
- **An excellent communicator.** He'll relate to the soldiers in your unit.

- **An effective counselor.** He'll listen to problems and recommend real solutions.
- **Another set of eyes and ears.** He'll help you focus on all aspects of a problem.
- **Seen by your soldiers.** He'll visit them at home, at the unit, in the hospital, in the field, and in the motor pool.
- **A soldier's chaplain.** He'll be tough when required and compassionate when necessary.
- **Your friend and advisor.** He knows the spiritual and physical demands of today's Army.

A good commander will:
- **Use** his chaplain.
- **Seek** his advice.
- **Honor** the confidentiality between a chaplain and a soldier.
- **Involve** him in unit activities and training events.
- **Encourage** his soldiers to get to know the chaplain.
- **Be** a friend to the chaplain.

A good reference is DA Pam 600-63-12, *The Army Health Program, Fit To Win, Spiritual Fitness.*

WORKING WITH THE INSPECTOR GENERAL (IG)

Don't head for the nearest exit when the IG walks in and says, "Hi, I'm here to help you." One of the IG's roles (besides inspections and investigations) is to help you and your soldiers. The IG and his team not only identify problems, but they also provide solutions. Work **with** the IG, not against him.

MEET THE IG: Seek out the local IG and learn his mission and how he can help you as a company commander. When the IG speaks, people listen. He can cut through red tape and solve your and your soldier's problems quickly. He may be shocked when a prospective company commander takes the time to ask his advice, but he'll be happy to answer your questions:

- How can you help me? How can you help my soldiers?
- How should I evaluate the overall status of my unit?
- What are the most common mistakes made by company commanders?
- What are the dos and don'ts for inspections at the company level?

FOSTER A GOOD RELATIONSHIP: Develop a good working relationship with the IG. Don't be apprehensive. The IG and his team are the experts.

BE CANDID: Don't try to cover up mistakes. Every commander makes a few. Learn from them . . . and from the IG.

War Story

Soldiers have a right to see the IG and request assistance on any matter. They can go through their chain of command or directly to the IG. One company commander had a policy requiring all soldiers see him before going to the IG. At first, his soldiers feared that he was threatening their right. Once he explained his position, however, the picture became clearer. To each soldier who saw the commander before going to the IG, the commander would say: "I can't help you with your problem unless I know what it is." He encouraged his soldiers to give him a chance to solve the problem first. If he couldn't satisfy the soldier's request, he ensured the soldier saw the IG immediately. Or, if the soldier wasn't satisfied with his solution, he also ensured the soldier saw the IG immediately.

The commander knew the IG would call him to find out the other side of the story. He knew his job was to do what was right for the soldier, and the unit. Sometimes, the commander could not help the soldier, but knew the IG could. This commander and IG worked as a team, taking care of soldiers.

YOUR SOLDIERS AND THEIR FAMILIES

The days of "If the Army wanted you to have a wife and family, you'd be issued one" are over. Today's Army is a "married" Army. Almost 60 percent of our soldiers are married, and when you include single parents, that figure goes beyond 60 percent. Don't neglect your responsibilities to CARE for your SOLDIERS and their FAMILIES. The word **C-A-R-E** says it all.

C oncern—You must be genuinely concerned about families. And that means knowing something about them. Talk with the families—don't wait for problems to surface on the MP blotter:

- Do you know how and where your soldiers live?
- Do you know how many soldiers have working spouses?
- Are their children cared for? Are day care centers available and acceptable?
- Is anyone sick in the family? (Visit a soldier's family member in the hospital.)
- Any particular problems with the children at school?
- Is your soldier spending enough time with his or her family?
- Are unrealistic requirements at work hurting family life?

You can show true concern for soldiers in your in- and out-processing systems. Make sure a soldier gets the time to in-process and settle his family before you introduce him to the rigors of work. Encourage your soldier's spouse to in-process with him and his sponsor. In-processing is the first opportunity a soldier has to start forming an opinion of your unit. *Remember, you never get a second chance to make a good first impression.*

Tip

A ction—It's one thing to talk about concern for your soldiers and their families, and another to show that concern. Provide all the help a soldier needs with a family problem. Determine his need early and ensure he receives continuous support throughout his tour of duty in your unit. If necessary, go to the battalion commander for help.

A classic example of supporting unit families is establishing an *ACTIVE* Family Support Group (FSG). This group takes care of your soldiers' families while your unit is deployed. When your unit isn't deployed, FSGs provide a support and communications network for your families. Your unit families actually establish FSGs. It's up to you to ensure support and cooperation **Tip** **from your leadership. Help your FSGs develop a structured organization with FSG representatives, a communication network, and unit links. Ensure they have access to meeting places, such as chapels, dining facilities, or the unit day room. A good FSG can improve your unit's readiness, because a soldier will be less concerned about his family while deployed. This group also can decrease problems associated with caring for family members. Consequently, setting up and supporting a good family support group is a necessity. Do it now!**

R espect—Always show respect for every soldier, regardless of his or her position, rank, or education. Jones may only be a private, but your unit needs privates and Private Jones is a part of your mission. The dignity of a soldier and his or her family is **not negotiable.**

E nrich—When your soldiers and their families leave your unit, they should be able to say their lives were enriched by the association. Use your imagination and consider every soldier's circumstances to provide memorable experiences for families.

War Story

A battalion commander in Europe organized unit trips for his soldiers and their families. Officers and their families went to Berlin, the NCOs and their families went to England, and the enlisted soldiers and their families went to Garmisch.

> *Each group sponsored bake sales and car washes to help pay expenses. For many spouses, the trips were their first visits outside the unit area. Ask your soldiers what they want to do, and then help them find a way to do it.*

Tip Don't forget, you have a family too. If you become so consumed that you have no time left for your spouse, will your spouse become enthusiastic about future selection for command? If your spouse is unhappy, what will your lieutenants' spouses be telling their "better halves" about future company command? When was the last time you spent quality time with your children? Families are important—including yours!

Do you recall the statement at the beginning of this section, "Don't neglect your responsibilities to CARE for your SOLDIERS and their FAMILIES"? Well, another—often forgotten—responsibility is to care for the single soldier. Yes, the soldier with a family receives more attention; the single soldier sometimes is taken for granted. He or she is too often the soldier scheduled for CQ on Thanksgiving and Christmas, simply because of being single and usually being around the unit area.

All single soldiers should have an "adopted" married family to care for them and for them to spoil. Just as you plan activities for families, plan activities for single soldiers. Most of your unit activities can easily include married and single soldiers. If a single soldier is appreciated, he'll *volunteer* for those dreaded details so a married soldier can be with his or her family. Your goal is unit and family cohesion and that goal includes everyone—married and single.

UNIT STATUS REPORT

The Unit Status Report (USR) is your assessment to your boss (and eventually HQDA) of your unit's combat readiness. It helps commanders at all levels allocate resources and identify factors that affect unit readiness.

AR 220-1, *Unit Status Reporting Procedures*, fully explains how to complete this report. Learn how to complete it and ensure your executive officer or another lieutenant also know how to complete it. You need a backup.

Tip **Since the Unit Status Report covers personnel, training, and equipment, include your orderly room NCO, training or operations NCO, and motor sergeant or motor officer in helping prepare it. Have them present their portion of the USR to you or your executive officer.**

Since its beginning in 1963, the practice or perception of submitting false or misleading USRs has been a continual problem for some. A few leaders, senior and junior, felt they had to manipulate USR statistics in order to look good. In so doing, they violated several UCMJ Articles and betrayed the officer's professional bond of trust.

By "fudging" or lying on the USR, a commander states he's better manned, better trained, and better equipped than he really is. If widespread, such reporting leads senior military leaders and the American people to believe the Army is better prepared to go to war than it really is. Thankfully, USR manipulation has been curtailed. An informal survey of Army battalion and company commanders in 1988 revealed that, as a general rule, no one had pressured them to alter statistics on USRs. Commanders felt that USR statistics reflected actual situations in the Army.

The most important thing for you to remember about the USR is to *TELL IT LIKE IT IS*! In areas requiring subjective determinations, be able to articulate the reasons for your determination.

A USR monthly review before the battalion commander is a common practice. Be prepared. It's easy for a battalion commander to **Tip** determine which commanders are involved in their USR preparation, and which aren't. It's embarrassing if you can't answer simple USR questions. It's also easy for the battalion commander to find errors, because she can compare all battalion units at the same time. A battalion commander will accept low ratings as long as they are justified and the company commander is working on the problem. The battalion commander also can direct a staff principal to assist a particular unit with a problem. Company commanders usually can become instant experts on the USR in only one or two sessions.

AMMUNITION ACCOUNTABILITY

Ammunition arguably is your most vital supply item. Weapons are useless without it; a tank without ammunition is merely a distraction. Not accounting for your ammunition can affect combat readiness . . . and your career.

War Story

A division ammunition officer made a division-wide reconciliation of unit basic load authorization documents, unit ammunition accountability documents, and physical inventories. One armor battalion had no fuses for its 4.2-inch mortar rounds (more than 400 of them). An infantry battalion and two artillery battalions had less than half the fuses they needed to make complete rounds. No one knew for certain how long this situation had degraded mission capability.

Ammunition accountability problems occur at all levels of command. Many commanders delegate their responsibilities and fail to have their subordinates do the inventories. Don't be one of them.

- Know what ammunition you're authorized. Each unit has a basic and operational load authorization based on its mission and size. Your property book will list both.
- Don't take shortcuts. Follow AR 710-2, *Supply Policy Below Wholesale Level*, DA Pam 710-2-1, *Using Unit Supply System Manual Procedures*, and local SOPs.
- Conduct the required inventory. You're required to inventory your ammunition, by lot, monthly. You may assign someone to do the inventory, provided that person doesn't do consecutive monthly inventories. However, you should personally inventory the ammunition quarterly to ensure that it's accounted for.
- Turn in ammunition according to directives. Turn-in procedures are an exact science. Demand your subordinates comply with these procedures.
- Don't mix and match your ammunition. Keep your training, operational, and basic load ammunition separate. Mixing causes accountability nightmares.

War Story

During a change-of-command inventory, the incoming commander found that property book numbers didn't agree with her physical count. An extensive investigation revealed the supply NCO had mixed basic load ammunition with training ammunition after a recent unit exercise. The unit supply officer supposedly told the supply NCO to get rid of the excess training ammunition "any way he could." Since the ammunition was mixed, the training ammunition actually was part of the unit's basic load. The supply NCO tossed the ammunition (basic load) into a nearby lake. The unit didn't recover the ammunition, even after dredging the lake for several days. Several soldiers are now civilians as a result of this incident.

- Get help for ammunition problems quickly. Your first stop should be the battalion and brigade S-4 office. If the expertise isn't there, call the ordnance folks immediately.

- Use the Amnesty Program as a last resort. The Amnesty Program isn't designed to bypass established turn-in procedures, but it can recover small quantities of loose ammunition. Only use amnesty, however, if the numbers don't add up after you've tried (and re-tried) formal procedures.

SECURITY AWARENESS

Don't let security awareness become important after the loss of a classified document or a Communication-Electronics Operation Instructions (CEOI) compromise. Thanks to our electronic age, security awareness is more important than ever. Stress the following points in your security awareness program:

- Take nothing for granted. Security awareness must never become routine. It's everyone's business.
- Pay attention to detail. Did you lock the classified document safe before you left?Did your driver turn in the CEOI after the field exercise? Were the notes you took at the last USR briefing with the battalion commander classified? If so, did you lock them up?
- Make security training classes productive. Keep the target audience alert.
- Purge your unit of all unnecessary classified material. The more you have, the greater the chance for a security violation.
- Don't sweep security violations under the rug. Take a firm stance when a security violation occurs.

Bibliography for Other Important Command Matters

AR 1-201, *Inspections*.

AR 220-1, *Unit Status Reporting Procedures*.

AR 600-9, *The Army Weight Control Program*.

AR 600-85, *Alcohol and Drug Abuse Prevention and Control Program*.

DA Pam 385-1, *Unit Safety Management*.

DA Pam 600-63-12, *The Army Health Program, Fit to Win, Spiritual Fitness*.

TC 22-9-1, *Military Professionalism (Platoon/Squad Instruction)*.

TC 22-9-2, *Military Professionalism (Company/Battery Instruction)*.

10. The Bottom Line

SO, COMPANY COMMANDER,

WHAT'S THE BOTTOM LINE?

The Bottom Line
for
Company Command

- LEADERS ARE STANDARD BEARERS. YOU'RE THE MODEL.

- GOOD FIRST SERGEANTS MAKE ROOKIE CAPTAINS GOOD COMMANDERS.

- A JUDICIAL ACTION ADMINISTERED FIRMLY, FAIRLY, PROMPTLY, AND CONSISTENTLY IS YOUR OBLIGATION—AND YOUR SOLDIER'S RIGHT.

- PEOPLE ARE YOUR MOST PRECIOUS ASSET; NEGLECT THEM AND YOU'LL FAIL.

- TRAINING IS YOUR NUMBER ONE PRIORITY. EVERYTHING YOU DO IS TRAINING.

- IT'S YOUR PROPERTY—IF YOU DON'T ACCOUNT FOR IT, WHO WILL?

- YOUR MAINTENANCE PROGRAM MUST SUPPORT YOUR TRAINING PROGRAM.

- DON'T FORGET THE KITCHEN SINK—KEEP IT CLEAN OR YOU'LL GET "SCRUBBED."

Abbreviations

AAM	Army Achievement Medal
AAR	After-Action Review
ADAPCP	Alcohol and Drug Abuse Prevention and Control Program
ANCOC	Advanced Noncommissioned Officer Course
AOAP	Army Oil Analysis Program
APFT	Army Physical Fitness Test
AR	Army Regulation
ARCOM	Army Commendation Medal
ARTEP	Army Training and Evaluation Program
BAQ	Basic Allowance for Quarters
BAS	Basic Allowance for Subsistence
BDU	Battle Dress Uniform
BNCOC	Basic Noncommissioned Officer Course
"Can point"	Cannibalization Yard
CEOI	Communications-Electronics Operation Instruction
CFX	Command Field Exercise
CID	Criminal Investigation Command
CIF	Central Issue Facility
CONUS	Continental United States
CO1	Enlisted Promotion Report
CPX	Command Post Exercise
CQ	Charge of Quarters
CS	Combat Support
CSDP	Command Supply Discipline Program
CSS	Combat Service Support
CTA	Common Table of Allowances
CTT	Common Task Testing

DA	Department of the Army
DA Pam	Department of the Army Pamphlet
DLOGS	Division Logistics System
DOD	Department of Defense
DSU	Direct Support Unit
DWI	Driving While Intoxicated
EDRE	Emergency Deployment Readiness Exercise
EO	Equal Opportunity
FAO	Finance and Accounting Office
FC	Field Circular
FM	Field Manual
FSG	Family Support Group
FTX	Field Training Exercise
GP	General Purpose
HQDA	Headquarters, Department of the Army
HTNR	Hometown News Release
ITEP	Individual Training and Evaluation Program
JAG	Judge Advocate General
LES	Leave and Earnings Statement
LRC	Learning Resource Center
MAIT	Maintenance Assistance and Inspection Team
MAPEX	Map Exercise
METL	Mission Essential Task List
MFT	Master Fitness Trainer
MILES	Multiple Integrated Laser Engagement System
MOS	Military Occupational Specialty
MRE	Meals Ready to Eat
MPL	Mandatory Parts List
MPRJ	Military Personnel Records Jacket
MQS	Military Qualification Standard

MTOE	Modification Table of Organization and Equipment
NBC	Nuclear, Biological, Chemical
NCO-ER	Noncommissioned Officer Efficiency Report
NCOPD	Noncommissioned Officer Professional Development
NEO	Noncombatant Evacuation Order
OCIE	Organizational Clothing and Individual Equipment
OER	Officer Evaluation Report
OJT	On-the-Job Training
OPD	Officer Professional Development
OPORD	Operation Order
ORT	Operational Readiness Training
PAC	Personnel and Administration Center
PBO	Property Book Officer
PLDC	Primary Leadership Development Course
PLL	Prescribed Load List
PMCS	Preventive Maintenance Checks and Services
POL	Petroleum, Oils, and Lubricants
POM	Preparation for Oversea Movement
PQR	Personnel Qualification Roster
PSC	Personnel Service Company
ROAD	"Retired on Active Duty"
SF	Standard Form
SIB	SIDPERS Interface Branch
SIDPERS	Standard Installation/Division Personnel System
SQT	Skill Qualification Test
SSA	Supply Support Activity
SSSC	Self-Service Supply Centers
STP	Soldier Training Program
STX	Situational Training Exercise

TA-50	Shortened Version of CTA 50-900 Clothing and Equipment
TAMMS	The Army Maintenance Management System
TB	Technical Bulletin
TC	Training Circular
TEC	Training Extension Course
TEWT	Tactical Exercise Without Troops
TMDE	Test, Measurement, and Diagnostic Equipment
UCMJ	Uniform Code of Military Justice
UMR	Unit Manning Report
USR	Unit Status Report
UTL	Unit Transmittal Letter

Index

Preparation for Overseas Movement (POM), 99
Prescribed Load List (PLL), 173
Preventive Maintenance Checks and Services (PMCS), 168
Primary Leadership Development Course (PLDC), 126
Promotions, 93-96
Property book, 150-151
Property Book Officer (PBO), 140, 145
Property records, 150-156
adjustment to, 152-155
PS magazine, 172

Range control, 110
Realism in training, 112, 132
Reenlistment, 90-91
Rehabilitative measures, 55-58
Rehabilitative transfer, 57, 64
Ross, LTG Jimmy, 151

Safety, 105-106, 112-113, 132-133, 189-192, 194
Salesmanship, 17
Security awareness, 214
Sensitive item inventory, 143, 149-150
Separation from military, 59-60
Sexual harassment, 49-50
Shop operations, 175-176

Short-range training plan, 117
SIDPERS reports, 79-81
Simulation training, 130
Single soldiers, 210
Situational Training Exercises (STX), 123
Skill Qualification Test (SQT), 122
Smith, MG Perry, 19
Sponsorship, 96-97
Standard Installation/Division Personnel Systems (SIDPERS), 79-81
Standards, 13, 35, 36, 43, 51
Stotser, LTG George R., 172
Subordinates, 23, 24, 52, 62. *See also* First sergeant; NCOs; Officers, junior
Supply
budgeting and, 156-157
company commander responsibility for, 137-139
inventories, 143-150
learning about, 139-141
property records and, 150-156
references on, 139, 160
unit training and, 141-143
accountability, ammunition, 212-214

The Author

Major General John G. Meyer, Jr., is an Army Military Police Officer with a distinguished record of service. His broad range of assignments include several commands and key staff positions at the Pentagon.

He held company commands in Vietnam, in a division, and in the training base. He also led troops as a battalion operations officer, executive officer, and Military Police battalion and brigade commander in Germany. He has been Aide-de-Camp to the Commander of the Army Criminal Investigation Command and to the Commander in Chief, United States Army Europe.

His myriad of staff assignments include Assistant Secretary of the General Staff, HQ US Army Europe, and action officer for both the Deputy Chief of Staff for Operations and Plans, and the Deputy Chief of Staff for Personnel on the Army Staff. He also was the Executive Officer to the Assistant Secretary of the Army (Installations, Logistics and Environment) and the Executive Officer to the Under Secretary of the Army. His most recent Army staff position was the Deputy Director, Military Personnel Management, Office of the Deputy Chief of Staff for Personnel, the Pentagon. His last assignment was Commander of the US Army Community and Family Support Center.

General Meyer is a graduate of Florida State University and earned a master's degree in Police Science and Administration from Sam Houston State University. He also is a graduate of the US Army Command and General Staff College and the Industrial College of the Armed Forces. He wrote this book while he was a Senior Fellow at the National Defense University.

General Meyer is currently the Chief of Public Affairs, Office of the Secretary of the Army in the Pentagon.

COMPANY COMMAND

The Bottom Line

Text and display lines composed in Melior
Title and half-title pages composed in Classic

Advisory reader:
Dr. William McCarron, East Texas State University

Editorial reader:
Major Doris P. Miller, US Air Force Academy

NDU Press editor: Edward H. Seneff
Cover design and artwork: Juan Medrano

Cover design advisers:
Catherine Zickafoose and Earl Young